SIMPLY
BETTER

ASCD MEMBER BOOK

Many ASCD members received this book as a
member benefit upon its initial release.

Learn more at: **www.ascd.org/memberbooks**

SUSTAINABLE
FORESTRY
INITIATIVE

Certified Sourcing

www.sfiprogram.org
SFI-00774

SIMPLY
BETTER

DOING WHAT MATTERS MOST
TO CHANGE THE ODDS
FOR STUDENT SUCCESS

BRYAN **GOODWIN**

Alexandria, Virginia USA

Mid-continent Research for Education and Learning
Aurora, Colorado USA

1703 N. Beauregard St. • Alexandria, VA 22311-1714 USA
Phone: 800-933-2723 or 703-578-9600 • Fax: 703-575-5400
Website: www.ascd.org • E-mail: member@ascd.org
Author guidelines: www.ascd.org/write

MⷜREL

Mid-continent Research for Education and Learning
2550 S. Parker Road, Suite 500, Aurora, CO 80014-1678 USA
Phone: 303-337-0990 • Fax: 303-337-3005
Website: www.mcrel.org • E-mail: info@mcrel.org

Gene R. Carter, *Executive Director;* Judy Zimny, *Chief Program Development Officer;* Nancy Modrak, *Publisher;* Scott Willis, *Director, Book Acquisitions & Development;* Scott Willis, *Acquisitions Editor;* Julie Houtz, *Director, Book Editing & Production;* Ernesto Yermoli, *Editor;* Sima Nasr, *Senior Graphic Designer;* Mike Kalyan, *Production Manager;* Marlene Hochberg, *Typesetter;* Kyle Steichen, *Production Specialist*

All web links in this book are correct as of the publication date below but may have become inactive or otherwise modified since that time. If you notice a deactivated or changed link, please e-mail books@ascd.org with the words "Link Update" in the subject line. In your message, please specify the web link, the book title, and the page number on which the link appears.

ASCD Member Book, No. FY11-9 (Aug. 2011, P). ASCD Member Books mail to Premium (P), Select (S), and Institutional Plus (I+) members on this schedule: Jan., PSI+; Feb., P; Apr., PSI+; May, P; July, PSI+; Aug., P; Sept., PSI+; Nov., PSI+; Dec., P. Select membership was formerly known as Comprehensive membership.

PAPERBACK ISBN: 978-1-4166-1295-7   ASCD product # 111038
Also available as an e-book through ebrary, netLibrary, and many online booksellers (see Books in Print for the ISBNs).

Quantity discounts for the paperback edition only: 10–49 copies, 10%; 50+ copies, 15%; for 1,000 or more copies, call 800-933-2723, ext. 5634, or 703-575-5634. For desk copies: member@ascd.org.

Library of Congress Cataloging-in-Publication Data
Goodwin, Bryan.
  Simply better : doing what matters most to change the odds for student success / Bryan Goodwin.
    p. cm.
  Includes bibliographical references and index.
    ISBN 978-1-4166-1295-7 (pbk. : alk. paper) 1. School improvement programs—United States. 2. School management teams—United States. 3. Educational leadership—United States. 4. Study skills—Handbooks, manuals, etc. 5. Success—Handbooks, manuals, etc. I. Title.
    LB2822.82.G69 2011
    371.2'07—dc23
                                        2011015515

20 19 18 17 16 15 14 13 12 11   1 2 3 4 5 6 7 8 9 10 11 12

SIMPLY BETTER

Acknowledgments

An undertaking of this scope is not possible without the ideas, input, guidance, and efforts of many individuals. I'd like to thank those who served lead roles in the eight research reviews that provided much of the research foundation for this book: Tedra Clark, Kerry Englert, Carrie Germeroth, Charles Igel, John Kendall, Laura Lefkowits, Monette McIver, and Laurie Moore. Others whose research, insights, and ideas are reflected in this report include Elena Bodrova, Ceri Dean, Jim Eck, Danette Parsley, and Tim Waters. Feedback from reviewers Sheila Arens, David Frost, Nancy Modrak, and Monette McIver helped to sharpen and strengthen this book. I also owe a debt of gratitude to Vicki Urquhart, my editor at McREL, and Scott Willis, my editor at ASCD, for their keen insights and guidance. Finally, I'd like to thank my wife and family, who graciously tolerated the hours I spent tapping away on my laptop to complete this project.

Without the support from these people, this book would not have been possible.

Introduction

I would not give a fig for the simplicity on this side of complexity, but I would give my life for the simplicity on the other side of complexity.

Oliver Wendell Holmes Sr.

Overwhelming and discouraging—that's sometimes how this business of improving schools can feel.

I spend a good deal of my time at education conferences, where I've logged many hours in exhibit halls. At most big shows, these halls fill warehouse-sized rooms and feature row upon row of vendors selling new gadgets, programs, tools, you name it—a veritable cornucopia of education solutions.

I often see educators roaming the aisles of these halls with furrowed brows, their heads swimming with new ideas from the sessions they just attended, now being confronted with a bazaar of products and programs, all claiming to deliver results for kids. Add to that the countless articles, reports, books, and blogs, and the whole overload of information can be overwhelming, if not entirely distracting.

In 2009, I was part of a team of researchers at Mid-continent Research for Education and Learning (McREL), a nonprofit education research and development organization with funding from the Stupski Foundation, that launched a major, yearlong effort to capture what's currently known about what it takes to ensure the success of all students, and especially of children of color living in poverty.

Hoping to wrap our arms and minds around all that has been written, presented at conferences, and offered to educators in the name of improving student outcomes, we eventually identified and read more than 1,000 studies and reports related to seven components of school systems and the learning needs of underserved students. After reviewing this body of knowledge, we compiled eight reports, which provide the underpinnings of this publication. Each report addressed one of the following topics: college readiness, curriculum, pedagogy, student supports, assessment, leadership, system diagnostics, and underserved students. (The reports are available as free downloads at www.changetheodds.org.)

While synthesizing and compiling this research, we arrived at an important conclusion: to improve the chances of life success for all children, educators and policymakers don't need *more* guidance; in fact, they may actually need *less*.

Distilling Simplicity from Complexity

In some ways, the countless studies, articles, and reports on education create a phenomenon similar to what radio broadcasters refer to as signal-to-noise ratio—a measure of how much the true signal, be it Beethoven's *Moonlight Sonata* or late-night talk radio, is corrupted by static. Like the crackles and whistles that break up the signal of a faraway AM radio station, the preponderance of data in the field of education may drown out the big ideas—the key underlying principles of what's most important when it comes to improving the odds of life success for all students. Rather than add to the noise, this book attempts to sort through the complexity of schooling to identify a handful of "first principles" that, when intentionally and effectively applied, transform school systems.

The goal here is not to simplify complexity into vapid platitudes. I'm mindful of the observation of H. L. Mencken, who once wrote, "There is always an easy solution to every human problem—neat, plausible, and wrong." Instead, the goal is to work through the complexity to identify key principles at the heart of what it takes to help all students become successful learners.

How the Odds Are Stacked Against Underserved Youth

The odds of success are significantly stacked against many students, especially those born into poverty. One measure of how well our education system is serving students is graduation rates, the statistics of which paint a grim picture:

- Nationwide, nearly one-third of all students fail to graduate with their peers (Bridgeland, Dilulio, & Morison, 2006).

- One-third of those who do graduate are ill prepared for either employment or college (Greene & Foster, 2003).

- Only one-half of black, Latino, and Native American students graduate on time from high school (Greene & Foster, 2003).

- In some urban communities, graduation rates are as low as 17 percent (Neuman, 2009).

For individuals, the consequence of these failures can be catastrophic:

- The poverty rate of families headed by dropouts is more than twice that of families headed by high school graduates (Baum & Payea, 2004).

- A dropout is more than eight times as likely to be in jail or prison as a high school graduate and nearly 20 times as likely as a college graduate (Harlow, 2003).

- Over a lifetime, dropouts earn an average of $260,000 less than high school graduates (Rouse, 2005).

- The life expectancy for high school dropouts is five years shorter than for college graduates (Commission to Build a Healthier America, 2009).

From Beating the Odds to Changing Them

Like Geoffrey Canada, founder of the Harlem's Children Zone, we believe the goal of U.S. educators shouldn't be simply to help a few kids beat the odds and make it out of poverty, but rather to *change the odds*, and to do it for all kids (Tough, 2009). The question is: What will it take?

Others have, of course, attempted to tackle this question. In the book *Changing the Odds for Children at Risk: Seven Essential Principles of Educational Programs that Break the Cycle of Poverty* (2009), University of Michigan researcher Susan Neuman identifies several early childhood programs, out-of-school interventions, and community support systems that have been shown to mitigate the effects of grinding poverty on student achievement. However, her book focuses on interventions that come from *outside* the school, primarily because she feels that schools have not been as willing to change and adapt to student needs as community-based organizations (Changing the Odds for Students at Risk, 2008).

Simply Better: Doing What Matters Most to Change the Odds for Student Success attempts to build on Neuman's work to include interventions that schools *must* perform to change the odds for students. The underlying premise is that schools should be at the center of any effort to meet the needs of all students, if for no other reason than they are where millions of U.S. students are currently educated. These students need better opportunities *today*. Thus, the approach of this book is to determine principles and practices that can be employed *right now* to change the odds for students.

Building on *What Works* to Identify *What Matters Most*

In this book, I attempt to go beyond merely identifying "what works." The problem is not that too few programs "work," but rather that too many only *appear* to "work." Several years ago, Wade Carpenter, a professor at Berry College in Georgia, counted 361 "good ideas" that had appeared during a 10-year period in the pages of the respected *Phi Delta Kappan* (Carpenter, 2000). After reviewing the preponderance of seemingly good ideas (which included, among others, whole-language instruction, performance assessment, block scheduling, looping, and de-tracking), Carpenter wrote the following:

> It's embarrassing. It really is. Not to mention depressing. These are only a few of the "good ideas" that were discussed in the pages of the *Kappan*—silver bullets that would enhance, reform, and even save American education.... It is embarrassing because all these "good ideas" have produced very limited gains. It is depressing because nearly all of them really were good ideas. But the results of all this research and publication have been less than impressive. (p. 383)

In preparing this book, I've also been mindful of what New Zealand researcher John Hattie calls the "hinge point" effect size of $d = .40$ (Hattie, 2009). An effect size is the measure of the strength or overall impact of a program or intervention being studied. Hattie writes that an effect size of .40 is strong enough for educators to see "real-world change" in student achievement (p. 17). It's also the point at which an innovation exceeds the average effect size of teacher influence on student achievement—that is, between $d = .20$ and $d = .40$. Using this metric, many programs and approaches that appear to work are actually no more effective than average classroom teachers left to their own devices. By using Hattie's "hinge point" as a cutoff, this book attempts to identify *what matters most*—those programs and approaches that stand clearly above the rest.

Finding the Touchstones

Over the years, McREL has conducted several meta-analyses and research syntheses to identify what works in a variety of areas—from instruction to extended learning, from school to district leadership. This research has appeared in such publications as *Classroom Instruction that Works* (Marzano, Pickering, & Pollock, 2001), *School District Leadership that Works* (Waters & Marzano, 2006), and *District Leadership that Works* (Marzano & Waters, 2009). These studies provide a foundation for this book as they do, in fact, call out many practices that meet Hattie's "hinge point" test.

By looking at what works in classrooms, schools, and after-school programs, as well as what works for at-risk students and school and district leaders, this book aims to identify key or "first" principles for changing the odds for students. Educators would do well to continually return to these "touchstones" to gauge the merit and value of their endeavors.

The What Matters Most framework (see Figure I.1) identifies those areas that, when addressed properly, are most likely to have positive effects on student success. Stated differently, they are high-leverage, high-payoff areas for school systems. Briefly, the components of the framework, which are described in more detail in the following chapters, are as follows:

- **Guarantee challenging, engaging, and intentional instruction.** At the core of effective systems are teachers who challenge students, develop positive relationships with them, and are intentional in their use of a broad repertoire of teaching strategies.

- **Ensure curricular pathways to success.** High-performing systems guarantee that all students in every classroom, no matter what their aspirations, are provided with both *challenging* and *personalized* learning experiences that prepare them for life success.

- **Provide whole-child student supports.** To help students meet high expectations, school systems need to provide cognitive, emotional, and learning supports to address a variety of student-level factors that

Figure I.1
What Matters Most Framework

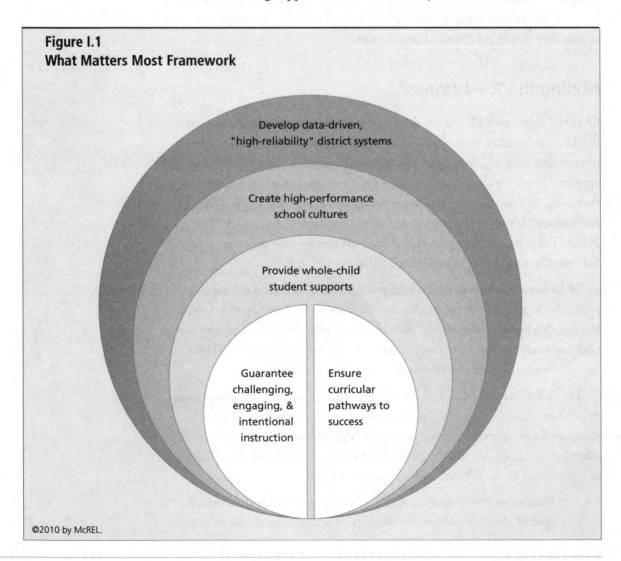

©2010 by McREL.

are crucial to their success, such as home environment, background knowledge, and motivation.

- **Create high-performance school cultures.** Effective schools ensure high-quality learning experiences in every classroom. At the same time, they develop a culture of high expectations for learning and behavior, which is an even more powerful predictor of student success than socioeconomic status.

- **Develop data-driven, high-reliability district systems.** High-performing school systems put data systems and processes in place to ensure consistently high-quality learning experiences for all students and follow established procedures for providing real-time responses to student failures.

These five areas may seem unremarkable. Indeed, one might look at them and say there's nothing terribly new about any of them. After all, haven't we known the importance of something like good instruction for decades? Perhaps, but what *is* remarkable is the powerful effect that getting all five of these areas right could have for students. For years, educators and policymakers have hoped to find some new approach, program, or innovation that can "solve" the challenge of how to prepare all students for life success. Yet the real solution appears to lie not in something *new*, but rather in a relentless focus on doing effectively what stands out from decades of research about how to improve student outcomes. In other words, changing the odds for student success does not require a wholesale reinvention of the system, or some new technology-driven innovation, but rather a clear focus on simply doing what we've learned about what matters most for raising student achievement.

If It's So Simple, Why Isn't It Being Done?

If we've known what works for so long, why haven't we put it into action? Here are some possible reasons why.

Urgent but Unimportant Concerns Distract from What's Most Important

Sometimes, even the most dedicated, thoughtful, and passionate educators can find themselves tinkering at the margins—wrangling over such things as what color to paint the school library or the merits of a lice awareness campaign—rather than focusing on what's most important.

At other times, educators may implement so many new programs that it's hard to sort through them all to know which ones work, and to what end. Several years ago, a team of Chicago researchers led by Tony Bryk encountered a school where the principal, in an effort to do what she thought was best for students, relentlessly pursued every new funding opportunity and program she could find (Bryk, Sebring, Kerbow, Rollow, & Easton, 1998). She sent her teachers to nearly every professional conference in the city, and filled her school with computers, books, and other tools. Bryk and his colleagues noted that "all of the activity and 'stuff'" even impressed a local TV reporter, "much as a Christmas tree laden with ornaments dazzles a child." In the end, though, none of the "stuff" did what it was supposed to do—raise student achievement. Efforts were fragmented and incoherent, and did little to "strengthen … the core of the school." Though the teachers were consumed with activity, they were not focusing on what matters most. Returning to the Christmas tree metaphor, the researchers concluded that "it was as if the branches of the tree sagged from the weight of all the ornaments, while the trunk was withering and the roots were dry" (p. 115). Being clear about what matters most can help schools become more conscious and thoughtful about each new ornament they place on the tree. Educators should ask themselves: Is this program or initiative worth it? Does it address a critical need, or will it just create a shiny new distraction?

Right Focus + Poor Execution = Limited Effects

As the old saying goes, the devil lies in the details. Some ideas, though simple in *principle*, can be extremely difficult in *practice*. (The Golden Rule comes to mind.) Indeed, researchers often have trouble discerning whether programs are ineffective due to faulty design or poor implementation.

Education systems are hardly alone in their struggles to do what "everyone knows" needs to be done. We might just as easily ask why automakers, airline companies, and banks do not apply the "open secrets" of success in their industries. Consider airlines: It's an open secret that, to remain one of the most profitable airlines in the nation, Southwest Airlines buys only one type of airplane to minimize training time and maintenance costs, does not offer "frills" such as movies and meals, operates out of second-tier (and thus cheaper) airports, and does not offer reserved seats, which reduces airplane downtime at the gate, thus maximizing revenues per plane. Other airlines have tried to copy these strategies but have never succeeded as effectively as Southwest, which logged its 37th consecutive profitable year in 2009 while its competitors rang up billion-dollar losses (McCartney, 2010). What Southwest has learned is that by focusing on the "big stuff" and getting it right—that is, by identifying clear, simple principles at the heart of an organization—it is better able to sweat the "small stuff."

Failing to Put All the Parts Together

We've probably all had one of those head-scratching moments upon completing a home assembly project when we've stepped back to proudly gaze upon our creation—only to notice that an extra part, with no purpose we can discern, is still left in the box. Sometimes the missing part goes by unnoticed. We hold our breath as our child tears down the driveway on his newly assembled tricycle and exhale only when we see that it works just fine. At other times, though, we discover that, like the seemingly insignificant distributor cap atop a car engine, one tiny, missing part can keep the whole thing from functioning.

When it comes to education, the five components of the What Matters Most framework are all necessary to ensure its best results—there are no superfluous parts. Sure, if we leave one out, the system will still operate—kids will continue to come to school, the bells will still ring, and the buses will still arrive in the parking lot. But unless all five of the areas are properly addressed, school systems will be operating at less than optimal levels. Worse, they may undermine their thoughtful, diligent efforts in other areas: For example, a team of great teachers delivering the very best instruction possible can still get disappointing results from students if they're being taught a curriculum that is poorly designed, sequenced, or aligned. And even the most engaging after-school programs can fail to deliver results if students are not identified and directed toward those programs.

At the moment, it's difficult to find many examples of school systems that have successfully put all of the components of the What Matters Most framework together in a consistent and coherent way. Certainly, there are examples of amazing teachers doing amazing things in their classrooms, of phenomenal schools producing impressive results for students, and of inspired communities wrapping their whole embrace around students to support their success. But these examples rarely occur in concert—or occur in isolated islands of excellence. Thus, the cumulative benefit for students of doing them all well is lost.

The power of a simple organizing framework, like the five areas identified in this book, lies in helping educators to survey the entire system they've assembled to determine whether they may have left any important "parts" still in the box.

What *Can* Be Done: How to Use This Book

As I noted earlier, the good news that emerges from our survey of research is that the powerful effects of the five areas of the What Matters Most framework suggest that changing the odds for student success *is* indeed possible. The challenge, of course, is getting everything right. Doing so requires more than just adopting a new program or following some rote, step-by-step sequence to success. It requires changes at all levels of the school system—something people have been advocating (with limited success) for years.

The ever-changing nature of school systems, of course, complicates matters. Each year, new students enter our schools while others leave, teachers come and go, new regulations are handed down and old regulations ... well, they never quite seem to go away. This unpredictability and complexity can make systems change in education a frustrating (some might say futile) enterprise. There are several ways this book can help to make our efforts more fruitful.

Staying Focused on What Matters Most

One way to free ourselves from letting urgent matters consume all of our time is to discipline ourselves and our organizations to spend more (if not most) of our time in the classroom and in faculty and school board meetings addressing what matters most. By calling out first principles for changing the odds for students, this book can help educators answer the question: "In light of the hundreds (if not thousands) of things we might do, are we doing what matters most?"

Consider the approach Southwest Airlines takes. The company clearly articulates a few simple strategies to drive its success. "I can teach you the secret to running this airline in about 30 seconds," Southwest CEO Herb Kelleher has said. "This is it: We are *the* low-fare airline. Once you understand that fact, you can make any decision about this company's future as well as I can." Kelleher gave the example of someone wondering whether to serve chicken Caesar salad on the flight to Las Vegas. His response to such a question is simple: if serving it "doesn't help us become the unchallenged low-fare airline, we're not serving any damn chicken salad" (Heath & Heath, 2007, p. 29).

By staying focused on a few simple principles, Southwest has been able to develop a company culture of people who believe in, internalize, and act on simple principles for success, thus getting the details right. Colleen Barrett, who became president of the airline after Kelleher retired, wrote in the company's in-flight magazine that "we often say that other airlines can copy our business plan from top to bottom but Southwest stands apart ... because of ... the collective personality of our employees" (2010, p. 12). Southwest employees' widespread commitment to superior execution of the company's business strategies is, in Barrett's words, the company's "secret sauce" (p. 12).

Reflecting on the Southwest story in their book *Made to Stick* (2007), Chip Heath and Dan Heath observe that "a well-thought-out simple idea can be amazingly powerful in shaping behavior" (p. 30). Getting the details right, *especially* in complex systems, appears to require simplicity. Simplicity, however, doesn't mean dumbing down, overlooking nuances, or making things easy. Nor does it mean plastering the walls with vapid platitudes that are the equivalent of encouraging people to whistle while they work. What's needed is an approach of *elegant* simplicity, one that calls out the core ideas of what's most important in order to help everyone understand, internalize, and do what's right, even when there's no supervisor or instruction manual to guide them.

Getting Everyone on the Same Page

As Heath and Heath note in their book, even the best-laid, most complex battle plans in military operations often turn out to be the equivalent of giving a friend move-by-move instructions for playing a game of chess for you: After only a few moves, the instructions are rendered useless by the unpredictable nature of an opponent's moves. In the heat of battle, so many unpredictable things happen that a well-crafted plan often becomes useless after about 10 minutes. Military planners have learned that complex operations don't require staggeringly complex plans with decisions that branch off in all sorts of directions. Rather, complex operations require a clear, simple statement of the commander's intent.

The What Matters Most framework and its component parts can provide a school system with the equivalent of a commander's intent, helping everyone to get on the same page about what needs to be done, every day, to ensure student success. This book can help everyone in a school system—from teachers to principals to district office administrators to policymakers—understand what they can do to ensure that this happens. Throughout this book, you'll find examples and resources to help you visualize how you can change the odds for students in your classrooms, schools, and districts.

Inspiring "Everyday Innovation"

What you *won't* find in this book are lots of step-by-step, how-to instructions. Southwest Airlines at one time "literally burnt" its thick customer service manuals and replaced them with "simple guidelines," recognizing that the key to its business lay not in creating prescriptive processes and guidelines, but rather in helping employees to understand what needs to be done and then trusting in their creativity and ingenuity to get it done (Braun, n.d.).

Similarly, the underlying premise of this book is that the key to changing the odds for students lies not in creating a raft of new rules, processes, or guidelines for educators; it lies in providing educators with a few clear, simple principles and then empowering them as professionals to use their creativity and professionalism to get the job done.

Encouraging everyday innovation may be, for some, a radically different way to think about school change and improvement efforts. It does not attempt to direct people's energies into getting their heads around sweeping new plans or adopting bold new programs. Rather, it recognizes the simple truth that improvement is, by definition, about doing things *better*. It's about everyone—including district staff, principals, teachers, food service workers, and other support staff—getting clear about what's expected of them and finding new ways, every day, to do what they already do, only better.

Checking Yourself and Your Organization: Have You Left Anything Out?

Entrusting employees to do what's right doesn't mean throwing out *all* processes or telling everyone to just do what they think is right. Southwest pilots, of course, still go through preflight checklists before taking off. In his book *The Checklist Manifesto: How to Get Things Right* (2009), Atul Gawande, a surgeon from Boston, describes in vivid detail the lifesaving benefits of using checklists to address complexity in such fields as medicine and aviation. For example, just as a simple, preflight checklist dramatically reduces airplane disasters, a simple pre-operation checklist, which includes asking the patient his name and verifying the procedure to be performed, dramatically reduces embarrassing, painful, and costly surgical mistakes.

Borrowing a page from Gawande, this book offers a series of checklists—items that people at all levels of the education system should examine to ensure they're doing the things that matter most. The point of these checklists is not to stifle creativity or ingenuity, but rather to recognize the complexity of education and help readers make sure they are addressing what matters most in their classrooms, schools, and districts. Moreover, these checklists are not offered as the final word on what to do, but rather as a beginning point for helping you think about how you might design and incorporate your own checklists into your classrooms, schools, and districts.

Offering checklists might appear to contradict my earlier point about the ineffectiveness of step-by-step instructions. Or perhaps you may find them a bit insulting. After all, how, you may ask, can you boil down what you do as a teacher or principal to a simple checklist? You can't. And this book doesn't intend to do that. As Gawande points out, checklists don't tell us what to do. They are not formulas. Rather, they help us ensure that we've got all the information we need, that we're being systematic about our decision making, and that we're not overlooking anything important. When it comes to endeavors with "true complexity—where the knowledge required exceeds that of any individual and unpredictability reigns," dictating every move "from the center will fail," writes Gawande (2009, p. 79).

People need to have the flexibility to use their own professional insights and creativity to develop their own everyday innovations and responses to challenges as complex as changing the odds of success for all students. At the same time, letting everyone operate as autonomous free agents, relearning mistakes and reinventing wheels along the way, doesn't make much sense, either. What's needed is "a seemingly contradictory mix of freedom and expectation—expectation to coordinate, for example, and also to measure progress toward common goals" (p. 79). Gawande adds that "ticking off boxes is not the ultimate goal" of checklists, either; rather, the goal is to "embrace a culture of teamwork and discipline" (p. 161).

Thinking Systemically While Acting Systematically

My colleagues at McREL and I arrived at the phrase "thinking systemically while acting systematically" a few years ago when considering the complexity of school improvement. We recognized that there are no silver bullet solutions or overnight success stories in education. Real change happens slowly, over time, when schools and districts build on successes, one after another, in a process of continuous improvement.

As Mike Schmoker notes in *Results: The Key to Continuous Improvement*, one of the biggest mistakes schools and districts make is "taking on more than we can manage" (1996, p. 61). Improvement efforts are most successful when organizations remain focused on simple changes, building on them as they progress toward a coordinated, systemswide response. Thus, it would be a mistake to read this book and plunge right into tackling all of the issues discussed at once. Rather, you should view this entire book as a large checklist of sorts that can help you to identify aspects of your work that you are already doing well, those you might tackle tomorrow or in the next few months, and those that could become part of a two- to three-year plan for classroom, school, or district improvement.

The chapters that follow describe in greater detail the simple, underlying principles related to each component of the What Matters Most framework. Ultimately, the key purpose of this book is to help you get to what Justice Oliver Wendell Holmes once referred to as "simplicity on the other side of complexity"—a place of clarity about what matters most for student success, so that you and your colleagues can be both *systemic* and *systematic* in your approach to changing the odds for student success.

1

Guaranteeing Challenging, Engaging, and Intentional Instruction

Imagine two students in early autumn. Like millions of other students across the United States, they enter new classrooms, where the usual first-day-of-school routines unfold. They find their way to their assigned seats or maybe scramble to sit next to friends, neatly arrange their new pencils and notebooks, write their names in their textbooks, and look up at their teachers, ready to learn.

At this moment, the two students are identical, performing exactly at grade level. Over the course of the year, though, a silent tragedy will befall the first of these two students. It's an all-too-common tragedy, one that happens to thousands of students each year. This student will steadily fall behind his peers. By the end of the year, he will be a half year below grade level. If his newly acquired academic deficits are not addressed, they may never go away. Worse, they may begin to snowball in subsequent grades as his confusion leads to frustration, apathy, and eventually dropping out of school.

Meanwhile, an altogether different experience unfolds for the second student. During the year, as the autumn leaves fall and then winter snow covers the ground, eventually melting around budding flowers, her learning accelerates. As she leaves school in early summer, this student has leapt a half year *ahead* of grade level. For her, school and learning have begun to "click" like never before, and new learning opportunities are unfolding. Though she was once unsure if she'd be able to attend college, it has now become her personal goal.

What happened to these two students to make their lives take such different turns? One simple variable: their teachers.

As Stanford economist Eric Hanushek (2002) has determined, the difference between a good and bad teacher can translate into as much as one year's worth of additional learning for a student *per year*. Highly effective teachers—those in the top fifth of all teachers—help students learn, on average, the equivalent of a *year and a half* of learning in a single year, while those in the bottom fifth only impart an average of a *half year* of learning.

Recently, the *Los Angeles Times* analyzed performance data of more than 6,000 elementary school students in the Los Angeles Unified School District to estimate the effectiveness of their teachers. It found that "highly effective teachers routinely propel students from below grade level to advanced in a single year" (Felch, Song, & Smith, 2010). Overall, students in the classrooms with the most effective teachers—those in the top 10 percent—ended the year 17 percentage points higher in English and 25 points higher in math than students stuck with teachers in the bottom 10 percent.

The effects of bad teaching tend to linger long after students leave their classrooms. In a groundbreaking study, William Sanders analyzed the achievement of more than 100,000 students and found that the residual effects of poor instruction show up years later in diminished student achievement scores (Sanders & Rivers, 1996). He also determined that students who have the misfortune of receiving a string of ineffective teachers for three years in a row scored as much as 50 percentage points lower on statewide assessments than those students who benefited from a three-year string of effective teachers.

Unfortunately, this scenario is common. Researcher Robert Pianta and his colleagues (2007) closely examined the educational experiences of 994 students from across the United States in grades 1, 3, and 5 and found that 9 percent of students received poor-quality instruction and emotional support in all three grades. (Conversely, only 7 percent of students spent all three years receiving high-quality instruction and emotional support.) And which unlucky students were most likely to receive poor instruction? Disproportionately, they were low-income students. In other words, the very students who stand to benefit most from high-quality instruction tend to be the ones most disadvantaged by poor teaching.

That's the bad news.

The good news is that teacher distribution and teacher quality are variables that can be changed. Thus, one of the most important ways that school systems can change the odds for students is to ensure that every child receives the benefit of a great teacher, every year, and in every classroom.

What Makes a Teacher Effective?

There's little mystery as to what makes one teacher more effective than another. After reviewing hundreds of meta-analyses on teaching effects, John Hattie (2009) concluded that "the current mantra, that *teachers make the difference*, is misleading" because "not all teachers have powerful effects on students"; indeed, he notes that "it is teachers' variability in effect and impact that is critical" (p. 108). Hattie concludes that "it is teachers *using particular teaching methods*, teachers *with high expectations for all students*, and teachers *who have created positive student–teacher relationships* that are more likely to have the above average effects on student achievement" (p. 126). Decades of research suggest that the following teacher behaviors, which serve as the touchstones for this chapter, distinguish highly effective teachers:

- **Highly effective teachers challenge their students.** Good teachers not only have high expectations for all students but also challenge them, providing instruction that develops higher-order thinking skills.

- **Highly effective teachers create positive classroom environments.** One of the strongest correlates of effective teaching is the strength of relationships teachers develop with students.

- **Highly effective teachers are intentional about their teaching.** Good teachers are clear about what they're trying to teach and then master a broad repertoire of instructional strategies to help students accomplish their learning goals. They know not only *what* to do to support student learning but *how*, *when*, and *why* to do it.

Setting High Expectations and Challenging Students

In 1965, Robert Rosenthal and Lenore Jacobson, in a now famous experiment, told a group of teachers that some of the students in their classrooms had been identified by a special Harvard test as being on the brink of rapid intellectual and academic development (Rosenthal & Jacobson, 1992). Unbeknownst to the teachers, the test didn't exist at all; the students had simply been randomly labeled as having special aptitudes. By the end of the experiment, many students who had been randomly labeled as special were demonstrating higher IQs than their peers—results that Rosenthal and Jacobson termed the "Pygmalion effect." The researchers concluded that, just as Henry Higgins's high expectations of Eliza Doolittle became a self-fulfilling prophecy in George Bernard Shaw's *Pygmalion*, teacher expectations can transform student performance.

In a review of 800 meta-analyses of education research, John Hattie (2009) notes that while some researchers have questioned the findings of the original Rosenthal experiment, 674 studies conducted since that time have confirmed its key conclusion: that teacher expectations do, indeed, have a powerful effect on student achievement.

Exactly *how* teachers convey their expectations remains a critical variable, though. For example, the effects of simply praising students—one obvious way that teachers might convey high expectations to students—appear to be minimal (Hattie, 2009).

Carol Dweck, a Stanford psychologist, has determined that praising students by telling them they are smart may actually have a detrimental effect on their achievement. Dweck and her colleagues conducted an experiment in which they divided students into two groups. They consistently praised students in the first group for their ability, telling them, "Wow. You got ... eight right. That's a really good score. You must be really *smart* [emphasis added] at this." The second group, they praised for effort: "Wow. You got ... eight right. That's a really good score. You must have *worked* [emphasis added] really hard at this" (Dweck, 2006, pp. 71–72).

The group of mostly adolescent students, according to Dweck, began the experiment "exactly equal" (p. 72). Yet afterward, the students praised for innate ability began to develop a "fixed mindset"; that is, they believed that achievement was based on innate smarts, not earned or developed through effort. These students began to reject more challenging tasks, fearing that if they tried and failed at them, they would no longer be perceived as smart or special. On the other hand, 90 percent of those students praised for their effort were willing not only to accept challenging tasks but actually enjoyed them.

Dweck concluded that one of the ways great teachers stand out from others is that they tend to have a "growth mind-set." They view achievement not as innate, but rather as changeable—the result of hard work. In contrast, "teachers with a fixed mindset create an atmosphere of judging. These teachers look at students' beginning performance and decide who's smart and who's dumb. Then they give up on the 'dumb' ones." On the other hand, "great teachers," Dweck writes, "believe in the growth of the intellect and talent, and they are fascinated with the process of learning" (p. 190). Dweck points to Jaime Escalante, the Los Angeles teacher whose story was told in the film *Stand and Deliver*, as someone who saw the potential in his students, regardless of their previous performance, not only to learn but to excel at calculus.

Exercising the Brain

If you were to announce to a personal trainer, "Sorry, I can't lift weights because I'm not very strong," your trainer would no doubt tell you that lifting weights makes your muscles stronger and thus able to lift more weight. What Dweck is saying, and what current brain research is confirming, is that the same principle applies to the brain. Like a muscle, it becomes stronger the more it's used.

Researchers at Carnegie Mellon University, for example, recently discovered that intensive remedial reading instruction not only improved the reading skills of struggling readers, it actually *changed their brains* by fostering the growth of new white-matter connections. These new connections appear to help students drown out distracting thoughts so they can focus more on reading. Marcel Just, one of the study's principal researchers, said that this and similar findings show that "we're not at the

Encouraging Growth Mind-Sets

In *Mindset* (2006), Dweck offers many examples of things teachers can say to reinforce the message that it's *effort*, not smarts, that counts. Here are a few:

- "You put so much thought into this essay. It really makes me understand Shakespeare in a new way."

- "That homework was so long and involved. I really admire the way you concentrated and finished it."

- "That picture has so many beautiful colors. Tell me about them."

The key to all three above examples is that they focus on children's efforts, not their personality attributes or traits (e.g., their ability to grasp Shakespeare when most kids don't understand him, their perfect score on a homework assignment, or their ability to draw rainbows, which could dissuade them from drawing other things).

So what about when kids fall short? Dweck recommends that teachers respond with the following sorts of phrases:

- "Everyone learns in a different way. Let's keep trying to find the way that works for you."

- "I liked the effort you put in, but let's work together some more and figure out what it is you don't understand."

Source: From *Mindset* (p. 178), by C. Dweck, 2006, New York: Random House.

mercy of our biology.... I think that's a fruitful way to think about life and society in general" (Roth, 2009). The bottom line appears to be that Thomas Edison's well-worn adage that "genius is 1 percent inspiration and 99 percent perspiration" is now being supported by modern brain science, which is finding that great minds can be made, not just born.

Building Strong Relationships with Students

Dweck has observed that great teachers both "challenge and nurture" their students. As an example, she cites Dorothy DeLay, the famous violin instructor (who counted Itzhak Perlman among her pupils). One of DeLay's students once remarked, "That is part of Miss DeLay's genius—to put people in a frame of mind where they can do their very best. Very few teachers can actually get you to your ultimate potential. Miss DeLay has that gift. She challenges you at the same time that you are feeling nurtured" (Dweck, 2006, p. 192).

In 1969, Judith Kleinfeld, then a Harvard doctoral student, traveled to Alaska "eager to do research that mattered, to find ways of improving education for children who were not doing well in school" (1972, p. 29). Hoping to identify which teaching styles had the most positive impact on Native Alaskan students, she spent a year observing classroom interactions between teachers and students in two boarding schools.

Over the course of the year, Kleinfeld identified four types of teachers. The first type she calls *traditionalists*—teachers who set high expectations for students but viewed developing personal relationships with them as outside their professional purview, offering little academic or emotional support to help students meet expectations. Kleinfeld described one such teacher as follows:

> Mr. W is a nervous man with a perpetually strained facial expression.... During the observation, Mr. W. stood behind his desk lecturing.... He placed a summary of the main concepts of the lecture, highly technical terms, on the board. The ... students dutifully wrote down the words.

> In a later interview, Mr. W. voiced serious concern for ... students and noted that their main problem in the class was vocabulary. They couldn't understand what he was saying....

Mr. W. mentioned, "[Some] students are afraid of me because I yell at them. Well, I do jump on them when they are slack on work" (p. 29)

The second teacher type Kleinfeld characterized as *sophisticates*—aloof and undemanding. The third type—warm but undemanding—were *sentimentalists*. Only those belonging to the fourth group—the *supportive gadflies*—were successful with students. Teachers in this group combined "high personal warmth with high active demandingness" (p. 29). In the classrooms of these teachers, students actively participated in discussions and were willing to work hard for their teachers, with whom they had developed a positive, mutually respectful rapport. In short, this group of teachers demonstrated the power of the old saying, "People don't care how much you know until they know how much you care."

In a later publication, Kleinfeld coined a new term for supportive gadflies—*warm demanders* (1975). Since that time, dozens of scholarly articles have used it to describe the widely affirmed quality of effective teachers: setting high expectations while nurturing student growth. Hattie's recent examination of 800 meta-analyses on student achievement lends further credence to this concept, finding that one of the strongest correlates of teacher effectiveness is teacher–student relationships. Hattie found that the top teacher–student relationship variables associated with higher levels of student achievement are as follows:

- Nondirectivity (i.e., encouraging student-initiated and -regulated activities)

- Empathy

- Warmth

- Encouragement of higher-order thinking

Building Relationships with Students

In the movies, relationships form easily, often during a montage scene while perky music plays in the background. In real-life classrooms, though, it takes much more day-to-day effort to develop strong bonds with students. Here are some tips for developing positive teacher–student relationships.

- Talk casually with students about their interests before or after class.

- Greet students by name as they enter the classroom. (This may be especially important for "problem students," with whom it's easy to inadvertently limit interaction.)

- Comment on important events in students' lives—for example, congratulating a student on a good performance in the school play.

- Consciously seek to make eye contact with every student in the room.

- Freely move about your room, deliberately seeking to move toward and be close to all students, especially those who are struggling.

- Use "get-to-know-you" activities at the beginning of the school year.

Although some of these tips may seem obvious, it's easy for them to fall by the wayside in the crush of daily events. It can also be easy for teachers to skip these sorts of

Continued on next page ❯

"touchy-feely" exercises in order to get down to the "business" of teaching. However, teachers need to recognize that these sorts of relationship-building efforts can make their job of teaching much easier, so it's worth investing time and energy in them.

Source: From *Dimensions of Learning: Teacher's Manual,* by R. J. Marzano and D. J. Pickering, with D. E. Arredondo, G. J. Blackburn, R. S. Brandt, C. A. Moffett, D. E. Paynter, J. E. Pollock, and J. Whisler, 1997, Alexandria, VA: ASCD.

This final bullet point—encouragement of higher-order thinking—bears highlighting. In the 1950s, a team of cognitive psychologists led by Benjamin Bloom developed a six-level "taxonomy" (later revised in the 1990s) for classifying intellectual behavior. By classifying learning from its simplest to most complex levels (i.e., remembering, understanding, applying, analyzing, evaluating, and creating), Bloom's taxonomy represents one way to measure the extent to which teachers are providing their students with intellectually challenging classroom experiences.

Over the past few years, McREL has collected data from more than 27,000 classroom observations that offer a dismaying glimpse into the level of instruction that appears to be occurring in the nation's classrooms. In well over half of these observations, student learning reflected the two *lowest* levels of Bloom's taxonomy: remembering (25 percent) and understanding (32 percent). Meanwhile, students were developing the higher-order thinking skills of analysis (9 percent), evaluation (3 percent), and creation (4 percent) in *less than one-sixth* of the classrooms observed.

Certainly, not all learning can focus on higher-order thinking; teachers must develop students' ability to recall and understand basic concepts before they can move on to more critical thinking. Nonetheless, the fact that so much of what goes on in classrooms appears to be focused on low-level thinking suggests that high expectations and challenging instruction may be the exception, rather than the norm, for most students.

A final point to be made with regard to teacher–student relationships is that they should not be seen as a substitute for, but rather as a *complement* to, setting high expectations for learning. For some students, especially those who resist learning simply because they want to have some control over their own activities, a little empathy and nondirectivity can go a long way. That's what Jeffrey Cornelius-White, a professor at Missouri State University, concluded after conducting a meta-analysis of research on teacher–student relationships. He found that person-centered learning—that is, teachers' displaying warmth, empathy, and "nondirectivity"—was associated with large increases in student participation and motivation to learn. He noted, in particular, that for students who are oppositional or resistant to learning, "avoiding power struggles through empathy and the encouragement of self-initiated learning seems to help" (Cornelius-White, 2007, p. 131).

However, Cornelius-White also observed that some students' resistance to learning stems from their simply wanting to avoid effort. For these students, no amount of cajoling, nurturing, or sweet talk will likely goad them into taking their studies seriously. Indeed, Cornelius-White found in his meta-analysis that a stronger student–teacher relationship "appears to have virtually no effect" in persuading students who are simply avoiding effort to try harder (p. 131). These students don't need more empathy or warmth, they need some "tough love" that helps them to overcome their own low expectations—or fixed mind-set—for themselves (for an example, read the sidebar about Marva Collins on p. 26). Instead of letting students think they're OK just where they are, growth-minded teachers tell it to students like it is, letting them know where they're falling short and then giving them the tools and support they need to step up their learning efforts.

Teaching with Intention

Conveying high expectations and building strong relationships with students, while essential to effective teaching, are still not, by themselves, sufficient: they are

---

A Resource for "Warm Demanders"

In his book *Teach Like a Champion* (2010), Doug Lemov, managing director of Uncommon Schools, a network of urban charter schools, lays out a taxonomy of instructional practices drawn from his observations of outstanding urban teachers. The no-nonsense teacher profiles from which these strategies are drawn exemplify the "warm demander" model of teaching—setting high expectations for behavior and learning while at the same time making it clear that they expect all students to meet these expectations and that they, themselves, are willing to do whatever it takes for their students to succeed.

Video examples of these teachers at work in the classroom are available on the Uncommon Schools website at http://www.uncommonschools .org/usi/aboutUs/taxonomy.php.

In *Mindset*, Carol Dweck describes the "tough love" teaching approach of Marva Collins, an educator in inner-city Chicago who took her 2nd grade students from well below grade level—struggling to get through the basic readers—to reading at a 5th grade level (e.g., Tolstoy, Frost, Shakespeare, and the like). The following exchange between Collins and an apathetic, openly defiant student named Gary, who, as this exchange opens, has refused to come to the blackboard, offers a compelling glimpse into Collins's no-nonsense, nurturing classroom demeanor.

> **Collins:** Sweetheart, what are you going to do? Use your life or throw it away?

> **Gary:** I'm not gonna do any damn work.

> **Collins:** I am not going to give up on you. I am not going to let you give up on yourself. If you sit there leaning against this wall all day, you are going to end up leaning on something or someone all your life. And all that brilliance bottled up inside you will go to waste.

> [*Gary relents to going up to the board but then digs in his heels again, refusing to work.*]

> **Collins:** If you do not want to participate, go to the telephone and tell your mother, "Mother, in this school we have to learn,

Continued on next page >

but two legs of a three-legged stool. The third leg of this stool is intentional use of instructional strategies. Without all three legs, the stool will not stand. It is not enough for teachers to believe their students can succeed and to show them that they care; they must also know what they're doing in the classroom. Or to be more precise: they must know *why* they're doing what they're doing in the classroom.

Going Beyond *What* Works: Knowing *How, When,* and *Why* It Works

Over a decade ago, researchers at McREL identified nine categories of instructional strategies that have a high probability of enhancing student learning (see Figure 1.1). Marzano, Pickering, and Pollock first reported these findings in their book *Classroom Instruction that Works: Research-Based Strategies for Increasing Student Achievement* (2001), where they noted that "no instructional strategy works equally well in all situations" (p. 8). Simply using the strategies at random will not raise student achievement; teachers must also understand *how, when,* and *why* to use them. In our work to help teachers improve their instructional practices, teachers often arrive at an "aha moment" when they come to understand what has been missing from their professional practice: intentionality.

By understanding *why* instructional strategies work, teachers are better able to put them to use. Effective teaching requires understanding not only what to do but also why to do it: Why am I giving a pop quiz? What am I hoping to learn about my students? Why am I breaking students into small groups? What am I hoping students will learn? Why am I giving a particular writing prompt? What am I hoping to have students demonstrate? As Figure 1.1 shows, understanding the *why* behind the *what* of the nine strategies reveals a simpler, smaller set of objectives that teachers must accomplish in the classroom.

Let's examine each of these nine categories of instructional strategies in greater detail.

Identifying Similarities and Differences. Marzano, Pickering, and Pollock (2001) note that the process of identifying similarities and differences appears to be "basic to human thought" (p. 14); attaching new information to existing knowledge and memories is, after all, the heart of learning. However, research shows that novice learners often fail to make connections between what they're learning and what they've already learned (Gentner, Loewenstein, Thompson, & Forbus, 2009). Moreover, what connections novice learners do make tend to be superficial (for example, identifying similar characters or story settings, rather than deeper, structural similarities in plot or themes). Thus, one of the key reasons—the *why*—for teachers to help students identify similarities and differences is to support their acquisition of new knowledge by helping them connect what they're learning to what they already know—familiar constructs, concepts, and processes.

Summarizing and Note Taking. According to brain researcher John Medina, one key to learning is actually *forgetting*—that is, weeding out extraneous information in order to make room for new knowledge (Medina, 2008). The process of summarizing information aids in knowledge acquisition because it helps students separate the wheat from the chaff of what they're learning. Note taking can also help students filter information (summarizing what's important and writing it down) and assist in the long and perilous journey that new information takes before finding a home in students' brains. Most new information that we process, Medina explains, gets lost long before it can make it into our

---

A Closer Look: A "Warm Demander" in the Classroom (continued)

and Mrs. Collins says I can't fool around, so will you please pick me up."

As Dweck recounts, that day, Gary started writing and never looked back. By the end of the year, he was analyzing *Macbeth* using references to Socrates and Greek mythology.

Source: From *Mindset* (pp. 200–201), by C. Dweck, 2006, New York: Random House.

Figure 1.1
The Why Behind the Classroom Instruction that Works Strategies

Strategies	Why They Work
Identifying Similarities and Differences	• Supports acquisition of new knowledge by linking to prior learning • Deepens knowledge with critical thinking (analysis)
Summarizing and Note Taking	• Focuses learning on important content • Deepens knowledge with critical thinking (analysis), review, and revision • Demonstrates understanding and identifies misconceptions
Reinforcing Effort and Providing Recognition	• Motivates learning through positive reinforcement • Motivates learning by developing growth mind-set in students
Homework and Practice	• Motivates learning through development of good work habits • Deepens knowledge through application • Demonstrates understanding and identifies misconceptions
Nonlinguistic Representations	• Supports acquisition of new knowledge through visual learning • Deepens knowledge and supports recall through visual learning
Cooperative Learning	• Motivates through "positive interdependence" • Deepens knowledge by "talking through" problems and strategies
Setting Objectives and Providing Feedback	• Focuses learning on important content • Motivates by personalizing learning • Supports acquisition of new knowledge by surfacing misconceptions
Generating and Testing Hypotheses	• Motivates by accessing "mental set" for problem solving • Deepens knowledge through critical thinking (evaluating, creating)
Questions, Cues, and Advance Organizers	• Focuses learning on important content • Motivates by increasing student curiosity, interest in topic • Supports acquisition of new knowledge by linking to prior learning • Deepens knowledge through critical thinking (analyzing, evaluating)

long-term memory. However, when we repeat or reinstate new information—within 30 minutes of first learning it, say, then again within a few days, and ultimately within a few months—we are far more likely to remember it. Thus, notes taken during class can serve as a handy way for students to review and reengage in material they've previously learned.

Reinforcing Effort and Providing Recognition. Carol Dweck's research makes a strong case for the value of reinforcing and recognizing effort. Good teachers understand this and know that the biggest *why* behind reinforcing effort and providing recognition is to help students develop a growth mind-set and intrinsic motivation to learn.

Homework and Practice. Although sometimes maligned, homework and practice have benefits for learning when teachers understand *when* and *why* to give at-home and in-class assignments. As Marzano, Pickering, and Pollock (2001) note, homework can serve two key purposes: letting students practice newly acquired skills and deepening their knowledge of new concepts. According to Harris Cooper, who reviewed research on homework, "Homework probably works best when the material is not complex or extremely novel" (1994). This being the case, it probably should not be used to *teach* new or complicated concepts. Homework and practice also provide educators with the opportunity to see where students are struggling and correct their misconceptions. However, according to Cooper, homework should not be graded or used as punishment, because doing so can rob students of one of the potential benefits of (and a *why* behind) the strategy: building intrinsic motivation to learn. One of the key benefits of students' doing independent work is helping them to see, as Cooper puts it, that "I must enjoy this; I'm doing it and the teacher isn't standing over me."

Nonlinguistic Representations. Medina (2008) writes that "vision trumps all other senses" (p. 221). Human beings are hard-wired as visual learners—a fact with profound implications for teaching and learning. Medina notes, for example, that "if information is presented orally, people remember about 10 percent, tested 72 hours after exposure. That figure goes up to 65 percent if you add a picture" (p. 234). Thus, the *why* behind the use of nonlinguistic representations in the classroom is pretty obvious: to tap into students' predisposition for visual-image processing, helping them to better recall new information later.

Cooperative Learning. Research suggests that when cooperative learning works, it does so because it gives students an opportunity to "talk through" material with their peers and thus learn more deeply than they might through individual reading or listening (Johnson & Johnson, n.d.). By talking through material, students become more conscious of the strategies they use to get to an answer and thus appear better able to retain new knowledge and skills. In addition, students can be more motivated to learn when a sense of solidarity develops among the group. These benefits of cooperative learning suggest that the *why* for this strategy is to help students deepen knowledge by processing it together and to motivate them to learn through what researchers call "positive interdependence."

Setting Objectives and Providing Feedback. Like summarizing, setting learning objectives focuses teaching and learning on important content, thus aiding knowledge acquisition by filtering out extraneous concepts. It also serves to build intrinsic motivation among students. In the early 1980s, Stanford psychologists Albert Bandura and Dale Schunk conducted an experiment with 40 elementary-age students. One group set "proximal" personal learning goals (e.g., aiming to complete six pages of instructional items during each class session), another group set "distal" learning goals (e.g., aspiring to complete all 42 pages over seven sessions), and yet another group set no goals but was told to complete as many pages as possible. Children who set "proximal" learning goals showed more motivation to learn (such as by solving math problems without being asked) and performed far better on a test of their skills than students who set "distal" goals or no goals at all. Finally, effective teacher feedback—that is, feedback that offers guidance on students' performance measured against clear criteria and explains why answers are correct or incorrect—serves to correct misconceptions before they become too deeply rooted. Thoughtfully delivered feedback can also motivate students to try and try again until at last they succeed—which is, after all, the very essence of a growth mind-set.

Generating and Testing Hypotheses. In his book *Drive: The Surprising Truth About What Motivates Us* (2010), Daniel Pink recounts the surprising findings of an experiment conducted by Henry Harlow at the University of Wisconsin in 1949. Harlow and his fellow researchers gave a group of eight rhesus monkeys some simple mechanical puzzles to solve. Almost immediately, the monkeys began to solve the puzzles without anyone showing them how.

Moreover, they actually appeared to *enjoy* solving the puzzles despite receiving no reward for doing so. The truly odd part of the experiment, though, occurred when Harlow and his colleagues gave the monkeys raisins as an incentive to solve the puzzles. The addition of the raisins, which Harlow thought would further motivate the monkeys to solve the puzzles, backfired. Once bribed with raisins, the monkeys began making more errors and solving the puzzles less frequently. The insertion of the external reward appeared to have undermined their intrinsic motivation to solve the puzzles. Researchers have since confirmed a similar phenomenon among humans, finding that people have a natural predilection for problem solving (which may explain the strangely addictive nature of jigsaw puzzles) and don't need external bribes to be persuaded to solve them. Students, too, are intrinsically motivated to solve problems. Thus, in addition to teaching higher-order thinking skills such as analysis and evaluation (or how to think like scientists in the science classroom), a key *why* behind asking students to generate and test hypotheses may be, again, motivation—that is, tapping into students' natural bent for problem solving.

Questions, Cues, and Advance Organizers. Questions that teachers ask in the classroom, cues (i.e., "hints" about what students will learn), and "advance organizers" (stories, pictures, and other introductory materials used to "set up" learning) can help students connect new knowledge with old and focus their learning on what's important. Moreover, questions, when asked correctly, can also encourage higher-order thinking among students by prompting them to evaluate and analyze new knowledge. Thus, the *why* behind this strategy is twofold: (1) to aid in knowledge acquisition by helping students connect new with existing knowledge and (2) to help

---

A Closer Look: Motivating with Classroom Mysteries

In the late 1980s, CBS aired a buddy cop show called *Houston Knights*. Many episodes of the short-lived series would open with a scene that *revealed* the killer or criminal. The show would then follow the hapless pair around as they tried to figure out what the audience already knew. The suspense-killing construction of the show likely explains why it ran only two seasons. It also offers some insight into why many lessons fail to interest students—and what we can do about it.

While researching what makes for good scientific writing, Robert Cialdini, a professor of psychology and marketing at Arizona State University, observed that good science writers don't come right out and reveal their findings. Rather, they develop a sense of suspense, posing a scientific quest as a mystery—for example, what are the rings of Saturn? Ice? Dust? (The answer is both—ice-covered dust.)

Inspired, Cialdini began creating mysteries in his own classroom. For example, to teach about the power of counterarguments in resisting persuasive appeal (a yawn-inducing topic if ever there was one), Cialdini poses this mystery: How did U.S. tobacco companies in the late 1960s reverse a three-year decline in sales and boost cigarette consumption while spending *less* on advertising?

Continued on next page ❯

Cialdini has since found that students stay in class even after the bell rings to hear the answer to a mystery. "All of us have heard of the famous 'Aha!' experience," he writes. "Well, the 'Aha!' experience becomes much more satisfying when it is preceded by the 'Huh?' experience. This is why the same student who will fall asleep reading vital course material will stay up until 4 a.m. reading a mystery novel."

The appeal of mysteries may also explain the power of such teaching strategies as cues and questions and generating and testing hypotheses to increase student interest. Used effectively, these strategies can tap into students' natural inclination to solve problems, puzzles, and mysteries and thus can hold their attention until well after the bell rings.

Source: From "What's the Best Secret Device for Engaging Student Interest? Hint: The Answer's in the Title," by R. B. Cialdini, 2005, *Journal of Social and Clinical Psychology, 24*(1), 22–29.

them deepen knowledge by encouraging higher-order thinking about it.

Reflecting on the *Why*

Adding the *why* to the *what* of the nine strategies might seem, at first, to "complexify" the elegant simplicity of the nine strategies. However, digging deeper into why the nine strategies work reveals some common themes and patterns among the strategies, which in turn suggest four key objectives of effective teaching:

1. To motivate and focus learning

2. To introduce new knowledge

3. To deepen and expand knowledge

4. To check for understanding and guide learning and reteaching

The example in Figure 1.2 describes how a teacher might use these objectives and the nine instructional strategies to design an intentional approach to teaching.

Intentionality: Beginning with the End in Mind

The idea of beginning with the end in mind is, of course, not new. Grant Wiggins and Jay McTighe have long extolled the power of "backward design"—starting not with textbooks or favorite lesson plans but rather with what students need to learn and then deliberately choosing texts, lesson plans, and other classroom activities to meet their learning needs (Wiggins & McTighe, 1998).

Carol Ann Tomlinson, a University of Virginia professor and arguably the leading proponent of differentiated instruction, relates the following anecdote of one teacher's epiphany regarding intentional instruction. After observing the teacher's class, in which

Figure 1.2
Teaching with Intentionality: An Example

Here's an example of how an intentional teacher might use the nine instructional strategies to fulfill key teaching objectives in the classroom.

Objective: Motivate and focus learning
Strategy: Setting objectives to focus learning on important content

When planning a unit for a 9th grade reading class, Ms. Jones uses a standard from the Grade 9–10 Common Core English Language Arts for Reading: Literature for her learning objective: *Analyze how an author's choices concerning how to structure a text, order events within it (e.g., parallel plots), and manipulate time (e.g., pacing, flashbacks) create such effects as mystery, tension, or surprise.*

To introduce these concepts, she selects Ambrose Bierce's "An Occurrence at Owl Creek Bridge"—a story known for its irregular chronology of events and twist ending—to teach plot structure. Borrowing a page from Robert Cialdini (see sidebar on p. 32), she introduces the unit as a chance for her students to learn some of the "secrets" of what makes one film a blockbuster and another a sleeper, or one book a best seller and another find its way to an editor's circular file. She tells her students that by the end of the unit, they'll have a chance to apply these secrets in writing their short story. Knowing that her students are more motivated to learn when they set concrete, personal learning objectives, she asks them to identify what they hope to learn during the unit.

> **Intentional teaching:**
> **A checklist for lesson and unit planning**
>
> **Motivate and focus learning**
> ☐ Learning objectives identified, articulated
> ☐ Strategy to interest and motivate students
> ☐ Feedback that encourages growth mind-set
>
> **Check understanding, correct misconceptions**
> ☐ Regularly check for student understanding and offer timely, criterion-based feedback
>
> **Introduce new knowledge**
> ☐ Strategy to link new to prior knowledge
> ☐ Strategy to access visual mode of learning
>
> **Deepen and expand knowledge**
> ☐ Strategy to practice, apply, and deepen learning
> ☐ Strategy to encourage critical thinking

Strategy: Using cues, questions, and advance organizers to generate student interest

Ms. Jones understands that students learn by connecting what they are learning to what they already know and that she can use cues, questions, and advance organizers to help students make these connections. She uses the following questions and ensuing class discussion as an advance organizer:

- Has anyone read a good book or seen a good movie lately? What made it good?
- Was it just the characters, or what happened to them?
- Did unexpected events occur that held your interest?

(continued on next page)

Figure 1.2 (continued)

Objective: Introduce new knowledge and develop understanding
Strategy: Identifying similarities and differences to help students access prior knowledge

Ms. Jones also knows that identifying similarities and differences is an effective way to help students connect new knowledge to existing knowledge, so she draws two columns on her smart board: one that reads "What makes a plot interesting" and another that reads "Examples from fiction and film."

Strategy: Using summarizing and note taking to support acquisition of new knowledge

Knowing that summarizing and note taking support students' acquisition of new knowledge by filtering out extraneous content and also helping them to later revisit what they've learned, Ms. Jones asks them to create the same two columns in their notebooks. Through a guided discussion with frequent checks for understanding, she has the class fill in both columns, identifying, with multiple examples from previous in-class readings as well as popular films and books, plot elements that make stories interesting, such as parallel plots, flashbacks, frame stories, complications, and plot twists.

Objective: Extend and apply knowledge
Strategy: Generating and testing hypotheses to develop critical-thinking skills

Ms. Jones knows that her students need to deepen their understanding of the new concepts they've learned and that her learning objective calls for critical thinking (e.g., "*analyze* how an author's choices…"). Thus, she engages her students in the higher-order thinking activity of generating and testing hypotheses. She reads to the class the first part of the story "An Occurrence at Owl Creek Bridge," in which the main character, Peyton Farquhar, a prisoner, is standing on a bridge, about to be hanged. She asks students to predict what will happen next.

Strategy: Using nonlinguistic representations to access visual learning and deepen knowledge

Ms. Jones understands the power of visual learning to deepen understanding and support memory, so after the class reads the story, she uses a graphic organizer to engage her students in creating a visual story line. They identify the events as they occur in the story—starting at the bridge, then flashing back in time to Farquhar's agreeing to sabotage the bridge, then jumping back to the present with Farquhar escaping the noose around his neck and fleeing his captors, before finally (spoiler alert!) returning to the moment the story started. Farquhar, the noose still around his neck, is hanged, his escape having been only a figment of his imagination. Using a graphic organizer, they rearrange the events in actual chronological sequence and show how one chain of events—Farquhar's imagined escape—branches off from reality.

Strategy: Using homework to expand knowledge and test for misconceptions

Ms. Jones understands that homework is best used to expand, practice, or apply knowledge. Having introduced several plot concepts, she now asks her students to read additional stories and identify, in written homework, the plot concepts they exemplify. She collects the homework and engages in a class-guided discussion of the plot structure concepts they found in the stories. This gives her a chance to see if students have misperceptions about the plot structure concepts they're learning.

Figure 1.2 (continued)

Strategy: Using cooperative learning to motivate learning and deepen knowledge

As a capstone to the unit, Ms. Jones wants to give her students an opportunity to engage in the higher-order thinking activity of *creating*. Over multiple class periods, she asks each student to write (and rewrite) a short story that demonstrates the elements of plot structure they've learned, followed by written commentaries in which students discuss, using specific examples, the key plot structure elements in their stories. Knowing that cooperative learning is most effective when it's framed around problem solving, holds students accountable for individual work, and occurs in groups of two to four students, she creates writers' workshops of four students, who work together to review one another's creative work against a rubric (see below) for evaluating plot structure in the stories they've written.

Objective: Check for understanding and correct misperceptions
Strategy: Reinforcing effort and providing recognition

Ms. Jones understands the importance of reinforcing effort, not mere talent or aptitude. So she provides each group with a grading rubric—one that makes it clear that she will evaluate their stories not on the basis of the students' innate cleverness but, rather, on how well they demonstrate the plot concepts they've learned and what they did to utilize feedback from their peers and teacher. She directs students to rewrite their stories and writers' notes based upon the feedback received from their peers and from herself. She grades the final stories and commentaries and to provide additional recognition, anthologizes them into a class collection of stories.

the teacher asked students to read a book, draw one of the characters, write alternative endings, and design a new cover for the book, Tomlinson asked why she had designed her lesson the way she did. After some probing from Tomlinson, the teacher suddenly understood what she had been missing: intentionality. "Oh my gosh!" she exclaimed. "I thought all they were supposed to do was read the story and do something with it!" (Tomlinson, 1999, p. 37).

Hattie's synthesis of meta-analytic research affirms the value of teaching strategies—when used thoughtfully to achieve clear instructional purposes. He concludes that students are most apt to learn at high levels when teachers clarify learning intentions for their students and themselves, select the most fitting strategies, and "provide appropriate feedback to reduce the gap between where the student is and where they need to be" (2009, p. 199).

Using the Touchstones: Putting Popular Teaching Approaches to the Test

In the introduction to this book, I noted that the key principles discussed in each in chapter can serve as "touchstones"—something educators can use to gauge the merit and value of their endeavors. Let's test that assertion.

If the principles of high-quality instruction that we've called out in this chapter—conveying high expectations, fostering meaningful relationships with students, and delivering intentional instruction—really are what matters most when it comes to teaching, we should expect to find that strategies or approaches that incorporate all three "touchstones" are effective. Conversely, those strategies that neglect one or more of the touchstones should fall short of the mark.

Let's take a closer look at three common teaching approaches to see what the research says about them and whether our touchstones help to explain why they may—or may not—be delivering results in classrooms.

Is Culturally Relevant Pedagogy Really Different ... or Just Good Instruction?

While sifting through research on what it takes to change the odds for students, especially those of color or in poverty, our McREL research team began with the following assumption: Given the volume of scholarly discourse around the need to adapt teaching styles to the needs of underserved students—an approach often dubbed "culturally relevant pedagogy"—we assumed that we would find significant evidence, examples, and guidance pointing to the need for teachers to employ a different, perhaps unique, set of *instructional* practices with underserved children. In other words, if one might normally use teaching strategy x—say, identifying similarities and differences—to teach a particular topic to nonminority or middle-income students, does the research suggest that the effects of poverty or culture dictate using a different strategy with underserved students?

After reviewing hundreds of research articles on pedagogy, we found very little experimental research to support altering teaching methods according to students' ethnic or cultural backgrounds (see, for example, Flowers & Flowers, 2008; Nasir, Hand, & Taylor, 2008). Judith Kleinfeld, the originator of the "warm demander" concept mentioned earlier in this chapter, has similarly concluded that "after more than 25 years of research on cultural differences in learning styles, psychologists have been unable to show that one method of teaching works better for children of one cultural group while a different method of teaching works better for children of a different cultural group" (1994, p. 151).

Kleinfeld acknowledges that some ethnic groups do occasionally display different ability patterns. For example, she notes that Alaskan Natives tend to demonstrate especially high levels of visual and spatial skills while performing less well on tests of English verbal ability. However, she concludes, "Just because different cultural groups have different cognitive strengths does not mean that teachers should narrowly match their teaching styles to these patterns of abilities" (p. 151). As evidence of this observation, she points to a study that she conducted early in her career.

The study was designed, she thought, to demonstrate the importance of aligning instruction with students' unique, cultural learning styles. Ethnographic research at the time suggested that Native Alaskan students had strong visual memories, developed perhaps to remember small visual cues needed to navigate the vast and seemingly monotonous landscape of the Arctic tundra.

So, Kleinfeld and a colleague developed two sets of lessons for teaching the classification of animals and their place on the food chain: one was verbally oriented, the other visually oriented. They delivered both lessons to Native and non-Native students, fully expecting to find the visual lessons boosting learning for the Native students. And that is exactly what they found. However, they also found that while the Native students "did learn more with the visual lesson … the Caucasian children benefited the same or more!" (p. 155).

Kleinfeld notes that similar efforts to identify strategies that are more effective with particular ethnic or cultural groups—for example, using cooperative instead of competitive learning with black students—have arrived at the same conclusion: The strategies tested are simply more effective for *both* groups of students.

That's not to say that teachers shouldn't attempt to put learning in context for students. Kleinfeld describes the experiences of one teacher whose first attempt to teach science to Native students in a remote Alaskan village consisted of a "boring lecture on calories and energy transformation" (p. 155). After getting to know his students better, he designed a lesson that asked students to visit a local steambath (an important fixture of village life) to observe the transition of water from solid to liquid to vapor. His students came back to class engaged in their learning and excited to talk about what they observed. One might conclude that the lesson worked because it was culturally relevant, but that would miss its real strength. On a deeper level, it worked because it connected what students were learning to their prior knowledge (namely, their experience with steambaths) and focused on developing higher-order thinking skills (e.g., analysis and evaluation). Both strategies are simply good instruction.

The bottom line: Effectively teaching all students does not require wildly different strategies; rather, it requires skillful and intentional use of existing proven practices.

The Curious Case of Differentiated Instruction

At this point, some readers may feel this chapter has given short shrift to the practice of differentiated instruction, which is aimed at meeting the needs of diverse learners and is an idea much in vogue in education circles. Carol Ann Tomlinson, one of the foremost proponents of differentiated instruction, writes that teachers who practice differentiated instruction in their classrooms

> accept and build upon the premise that learners differ in important ways. Thus, they also accept and act on the premise that teachers must be ready to engage students in instruction through different modalities [learning styles], by appealing to differing interests, and by using varied rates of instruction along with varied degrees of complexity. (1999, p. 8)

The logic behind this statement seems airtight. For years, such psychologists as Howard Gardner (2006) have contended that people learn in different ways. Some are visual learners, others are bodily-kinesthetic or linguistic learners, and so on. Each student, the theory goes, has a preferred learning style and comes to school every day with a unique set of prior knowledge and skills. Following this logic, the best response to this diversity of learning styles and aptitudes is for teachers to differentiate instruction, teaching students in ways that match their individual readiness levels and learning styles.

It all seems very logical, but there's one problem: To date, no empirical evidence exists to confirm that the total package of differentiated instruction (i.e., conducting ongoing assessments of student abilities, identifying appropriate content and instructional strategies based on those abilities, using flexible grouping arrangements for students, and varying how students can demonstrate proficiency in their learning) has a positive impact on student achievement (Hall, 2002).

One reason for this lack of evidence may simply be that no large-scale, scientific study of differentiated instruction has yet been conducted. And as any researcher will tell you, the absence of evidence is not evidence of absence. The lack of research itself may be due to the fact that differentiated instruction is such a large undertaking that it's difficult to implement well and thus difficult to study well. Indeed, some of Carol Ann Tomlinson's own research has found that even in those schools that claimed to be implementing differentiated instruction, few teachers appeared to be opting for differentiation in any form (Tomlinson, Moon, & Callahan, 1998).

Another explanation, however, could be that, while seemingly logical, differentiated instruction is based on some flawed premises. Some of the underpinnings of differentiated instruction, including adapting instruction to student abilities, aligning teaching to student learning styles, and providing instruction based upon individual students' interests, have yet to be confirmed by careful research. Here are a few salient research findings that Hattie (2009) cites:

- A meta-analysis of 61 studies of "aptitude–treatment interactions"— that is, grouping students according to ability and providing them with appropriate instructional support—found that these interventions provide more benefit to higher-achieving students than to lower-achieving ones and, thus, may exacerbate achievement gaps (p. 194).

- More than 400 studies found that aligning instruction to student learning styles has effects only slightly above what would be expected from normal teaching. And even these moderate effect sizes are in doubt according to Hattie, who notes serious methodological flaws with many of them. One concern with adapting instruction to learning styles, according to a pair of researchers who conducted a meta-analysis of 39 studies, is the "considerable overlap" in individual learning styles, which calls into question whether reported learning style preferences "could really be deemed preferences" at all (Kavale & Forness, 1987; cited in Hattie, 2009, p. 195).

- Six hundred studies of individualized instruction (i.e., instruction based on students' individual interests and past learning experiences) found these efforts to be "only slightly better than regular classroom instruction" (Hattie, 2009, p. 198).

The Trouble with Multiple Intelligences and Learning Styles

In his book *Why Don't Students Like School?*, cognitive psychologist Daniel Willingham observes that "children are more alike than different in terms of how they think and learn," adding that, "as far as scientists have been able to determine, there are not categorically different types of learners" (Willingham, 2009, pp. 113–114). He cautions, for example, against assuming that just because a student is naturally gifted in music he should be taught commas by being asked to write a song about them or that a child with bodily-kinesthetic aptitude should be asked to contort herself into the shape of a comma.

Willingham notes that Howard Gardner himself, the father of multiple intelligences theory, "disavows this idea, and he's right to do so" (p. 125). The problem with this line of thinking is that these different abilities—whether it's musical talent or being physically coordinated—have nothing to do with learning about commas. Similarly, "mathematical concepts have to be learned mathematically and skill in music won't help," writes Willingham (p. 125). So too, one might add, a baseball coach is unlikely to help a child with a weak arm (but who is good at math) make a better throw from third base to first base by asking him to write mathematical formulas of an orb in flight.

So what does all this mean? Is differentiated instruction a bad practice? Should teachers who are having success with it in their classrooms (and, undoubtedly, there are many) stop doing it?

Not at all.

These findings don't imply that differentiated instruction (or approaches similar to it) never works, just that it doesn't work *consistently*. Indeed, Willingham himself writes in a passage on this point that bears repeating:

> I am not saying that teachers should not differentiate instruction. I hope and expect that they do. But when they do, they should know that scientists cannot offer any help. It would be wonderful if scientists had identified categories of students along with varieties of instruction best suited to each category, but after a great deal of effort, they have not found such types, and I, like many others, suspect they don't exist. (p. 126)

So what's one to do with students of different abilities? Certainly, everyday teachers face the challenge of trying to educate children of different abilities. In a single classroom, a teacher is likely to have students with learning disabilities grouped with students who have been identified as gifted and talented. Those differences are impossible to ignore. Teachers, no doubt, often find that when they teach a lesson, not all kids immediately grasp the content the first time around—maybe a quarter, a third, or even half of the students don't get it.

The point to draw from the research here is that learning style differences are unlikely to explain why those students didn't comprehend what was being taught the first time around. Moreover, given the lack of research to support learning style preferences, there's no reason to label or group students according to these so-called abilities or design lessons specifically for them.

Certainly, providing math manipulatives that illustrate volume or more visual ways of presenting cell mitosis can help struggling students better understand these concepts. It's likely, though, that these techniques will help *all* students. The fact that some higher-performing students may bring to the classroom more background knowledge, vocabulary, or motivation probably goes a long way toward explaining why they may understand the concept of volume when it's taught in an more abstract way (i.e., "length times height times width equals volume"). This doesn't mean, however, that they won't also be more likely to understand and remember a concept when they encounter it in a more visual or tactile way.

Educators might still reasonably embrace differentiated instruction, with the caveat that it's not easy to do well. That appears to be the conclusion of a recent practice guide from the What Works Clearinghouse on implementing Response to Intervention to improve students' reading abilities. The guide cites the "low level" of evidence for differentiated instruction, yet still calls teachers to use the approach in their classrooms (What Works Clearinghouse, 2009, p. 17).

The What Works Clearinghouse report notes, however, that there is *moderate* evidence (that is, a number of high-quality correlational studies) that supports the practice of regularly screening students and monitoring their progress. And *strong* evidence exists from scientifically based research to encourage the practice of placing students who are falling behind in small, homogeneous groups where they receive one to three hours per week of intensive, supplemental instruction, including one-on-one tutoring (What Works Clearinghouse, 2009). Bear in mind that these groupings are not permanent labels applied to students—they are based on real-time assessments of how students are learning and should be reconfigured regularly when students demonstrate that they no longer need the extra support.

The Bottom Line: Differentiation in Moderation

One challenge, of course, in writing about differentiated instruction is that most likely, if you ask 10 teachers to define it, you'll probably get 10 different definitions of what it is. For some, it's simply the practice of teaching all students well the first time, checking for student understanding with formative assessments, identifying those who are falling behind, and providing them with some additional instruction. Research from the What Works Clearinghouse practice guide suggests that this is a prudent approach to differentiate instruction.

Some advocates of differentiated instruction, however, call for something a bit more complicated—for example, creating different options for different learning styles (e.g., verbal-linguistic, visual-spatial, logical-mathematical, intrapersonal) based on Howard Gardner's multiple intelligences theory. As we'll see more in the next chapter on curriculum, such tweaks or infusion of student choice in the curriculum may provide some benefit in terms of motivation. Some students may find it more interesting to use a Venn diagram to compare and contrast plants and animals, for instance, while others may feel more inclined to write about their "life as a plant" (Tomlinson & Cunningham Eidson, 2003).

So if experienced teachers wish to infuse student choices into their lesson plans and feel confident that each choice will require students to demonstrate similar levels of learning, they might reasonably get a little fancy, so to speak, with their lessons. Students may even benefit some from these extra flourishes. However, for some teachers, especially beginning teachers, adding this layer of complexity to teaching may feel like attempting to bounce down a treacherous, double-black diamond ski slope meant for experts when they've only just recently made their way off the bunny hill. For these educators, teaching is complicated enough without adding the additional, and, research would say, unnecessary, burden of trying to adjust instruction to students' so-called learning styles.

The bottom line is this: yes, teachers should differentiate the *intensity* of instruction according to student needs and mastery of content. They can, however, safely disabuse themselves of feeling obliged to adapt every lesson to differences in students' learning styles. The former, simpler approach to differentiation will do just fine.

The Ugly Duckling: Direct Instruction

John Hattie (2009) writes that he often finds his teacher education students have been "indoctrinated with the mantra 'constructivism good, direct instruction bad,' and are thus, stunned, if not indignant, when they learn that more than 300 studies of Direct Instruction have found the approach to be among one of the more effective in teaching" (p. 204). (It should be noted here, though, that only *one* study of Direct Instruction has measured up to the high bar of the What Works Clearinghouse, meeting the Clearinghouse's exacting standards for medical-style research complete with random experimental and control groups; this study, which examined the impact of Direct Instruction on 164 special education preschool and kindergarten children, found only small effects for the approach with its limited sample of students [What Works Clearinghouse, 2007]).

Hattie notes that contrary to popular conception, Direct Instruction (with capital letters, as in the program developed by Dr. Siegfried Engelmann, Dr.

Wesley Becker, and colleagues) is *not* simply didactic instruction or a teacher droning on in the front of the room—think the monotone lecture on the Hawley-Smoot Tariff Act from Ben Stein's character in the 1980s' comedy *Ferris Bueller's Day Off.* Rather, Direct Instruction is an intensely *intentional* process of instruction that involves teachers' becoming clear upfront about learning objectives, making them transparent to students, demonstrating them through modeling, monitoring student progress by moving around the room and constantly interacting with students, giving students opportunities for independent practice, and pulling the entire lesson together with a thoughtful "closure" that helps students make sense of what they've learned.

In contrast to these positive findings, researchers have found that less-structured and more student-guided approaches to instruction can be harmful for struggling students. One analysis of 70 studies conducted by Richard Clark, a researcher at the University of Southern California, found several experiments in which lower-aptitude students taught with less-guided or -structured instructional methods actually tested significantly *lower* on post-test than pre-test measures. In other words, they experienced a loss of learning while exposed to unguided instruction. Higher-ability students, on the other hand, achieve at higher rates with less-structured instruction, presumably because they have already acquired their own effective learning techniques.

In unusually strong language for the staid, equivocating world of peer-reviewed journals, Clark and his colleagues, Paul Kirschner and John Sweller, conclude that "after a half-century of advocacy associated with instruction using minimal guidance, it appears that there is no body of research supporting the technique." They add, "In so far as there is any evidence from controlled studies, it almost uniformly supports direct, strong instructional guidance rather than constructivist-based minimal guidance during the instruction of novice to intermediate learners" (Kirschner, Sweller, & Clark, 2006, p. 83).

At this point, astute readers may wonder: "Wait, didn't you say earlier that *nondirectivity* is one of the teacher characteristics most strongly correlated with higher levels of achievement? But now you're saying that Direct Instruction works. So which is it? Directive or nondirective?"

Admittedly, this is the kind of conflicting guidance that drives educators crazy and may cause them to hate research. But there is less conflict here than may appear on the surface. It all has to do, again, with intentionality—namely, what kinds of knowledge and skills we're trying to teach to students.

Research suggests that direct, teacher-led instructional approaches work best when the purpose is to introduce *new knowledge* to students. For example, rather than let students flail about trying to rediscover what Pythagoras figured out centuries ago about triangles, it's best simply to teach them that if they want to know the length of a right triangle's hypotenuse, $A^2 + B^2 = C^2$ works every time. A meta-analysis of 15 scientifically rigorous research studies of the effects of various mathematics instruction techniques on low-achieving students conducted by Scott Baker, Russell Gersten, and Dae-Sik Lee confirms this: They found strong effects for teacher-led instruction in mathematics ($d = .58$) and negligible effects for teachers who emphasized real-world applications of mathematics ($d = .01$). They concluded that "low achievers seem not to do well at authentic problem solving and discussion of mathematical concepts without solid preparation in the underlying mathematical foundations" (Baker, Gersten, & Lee, 2002, p. 68).

That's not to say, of course, that a teacher wouldn't use real-world applications to generate student interest in the topic—showing, for example, why a carpenter, surveyor, or astrophysicist might be interested in determining the length of a triangle's hypotenuse. The point here, though, is simple and commonsensical: When you need to teach new knowledge to students, it's best simply to *teach* it to them.

Cognitive psychologists also know that new knowledge exists in a fragile state in students' minds. A teacher can't simply throw out a new idea and hope it sticks. That's where application, practice, and higher-order thinking come into play—to help students deepen their knowledge, attaching it to their previous knowledge and applying it to novel situations that are meaningful to them. Less-directive, problem-solving approaches give students the opportunity they need to practice and apply their new knowledge. Just as we've all experienced suddenly turning into misspelling, ungrammatical dolts when someone watches over our shoulders as we type, students need some room to experiment and problem solve independently to deepen their understanding of new knowledge. That's where some nondirectivity can be helpful.

Incidentally, less-directive opportunities for independent practice are, in fact, built into Direct Instruction methods. Direct Instruction advocates themselves point out that neglecting to give students opportunities for independent practice is usually to blame when students are unable to recall information later or cannot apply their learning to new or novel situations (Hollingsworth & Ybarra, 2009). So, in the end, it appears that both directive and nondirective approaches are effective—when applied to proper ends and at proper times in the learning cycle.

That thought returns us to the heading of this section. We're all familiar with the story of the ugly duckling—the cygnet that's seen as ugly when it's among other ducks but grows into a beautiful swan. Like the ugly duckling, directive instruction has taken its share of abuse in academia and teacher education programs—probably because the method and its purposes are not fully understood. But when properly implemented and understood, Direct Instruction (the formal method) specifically, and teacher-directive instruction techniques more generally speaking, can have a powerful effect on student learning.

Using the Touchstones to Make Sense of the Data

So what are we to make of all this?

Three popular approaches—culturally relevant pedagogy, differentiated instruction, and constructivism—that remain in vogue in education circles don't have much solid research evidence to commend them. On the other hand, the ordinary and sometimes disparaged Direct Instruction approach has a large body of evidence (albeit not yet *scientifically based* evidence) to support it. Our three touchstones may help to explain why this may be the case.

First, in the case of Direct Instruction, by compelling teachers to set clear, challenging learning objectives, engage with students to monitor their progress, and use teaching strategies clearly tied to learning outcomes, Direct Instruction may, in effect, compel teachers to demonstrate the touchstones of effective teaching:

- **Setting high expectations and delivering challenging instruction.** Teacher expectations for students have a powerful influence on student achievement. The best teachers see intelligence not as something that is innate to, or fixed within, students but as something that can be nurtured and developed.

- **Fostering engaging learning environments and meaningful relationships with students.** Effective teachers are *warm demanders,* pressing students to achieve at high levels while developing strong, nurturing relationships with them.

- **Intentionally matching instructional strategies to learning goals.** The best teachers are clear about what they are trying to teach to students. They consistently monitor student progress toward learning goals and use appropriate teaching strategies to close the gap between what students know and what they are expected to learn.

This is not to say that Direct Instruction is the only approach that works in the classroom. To the contrary; as I noted in the introduction, the purpose of this book is not to propose lockstep, one-size-fits-all solutions, but instead to call out the deep principles of success in classrooms and schools. The point here, then, is simply to say that the documented success of Direct Instruction is likely the result of its helping teachers to attend to the things that matter most in the classroom.

Moreover, holding up other instructional approaches to the touchstones may help explain why they fall short—if not in theory, at least in practice. Indeed, the real message to draw from the dearth of evidence supporting differentiated instruction and culturally relevant pedagogy may be this: The extent to which teachers differentiate instruction in their classrooms is *not* a key variable in student success. Differentiated instruction and culturally relevant pedagogy may be more of a means to an end, a way to address these three touchstones of teacher success.

Teachers who exemplify all three of the aforementioned touchstones of good instruction will almost assuredly deliver great results for students. Take away any one of them and teacher effectiveness, along with student success, will decrease. For example, if teachers differentiate instruction yet fail to develop strong nurturing relationships with students, they won't be as successful as teachers who differentiate instruction *and* develop positive relationships with students. Similarly, if they deliver what they believe to be more culturally relevant pedagogy but set low expectations for learning, they're unlikely to raise student achievement. On the other hand, when differentiated instruction, culturally relevant pedagogy, or any other instructional approach *does* work, it's likely because teachers are delivering instruction that reflects all three touchstones.

In the end, the simple takeaway message from this chapter is this: Simply nurturing kids and "loving them up" won't produce learning. Nor will simply setting high expectations. Teachers must do both—challenge *and* nurture students. At the same time, they must know *why* they're doing *what* they're doing in the classroom. Take away any one of the touchstones—regardless of the instructional approach teachers may be using in the classroom—and you'll get mediocre results at best. Put them all together and you're bound to succeed.

2

Ensuring Curricular Pathways to Success

In the preceding chapter, I established that providing all students with a great teacher is critical to improving their odds for success. The question remains, however, What should great teachers teach? What curriculum should they follow to provide their students with the knowledge and skills they need to be successful in life?

This question, as it turns out, is one that has dogged educators for centuries—at least since the time of the ancient Greek philosophers.

An Age-Old Question

Socrates, perhaps the most famous educator of the ancient world, surveyed ancient Athens and determined that what passed for knowledge with most citizens was really just trivial information—a far cry from true wisdom (Brickhouse & Smith, 2000). So as he walked about the stone streets of the city with his eager band of students, instead of directly teaching them practical knowledge and skills (such as how to plumb a building), he taught them, in the nondogmatic style that now bears his name, many of the mental habits that today we call higher-order thinking skills—the ability, for example, to analyze, think logically, and question the assumptions of others, even those in positions of authority. We all know, of course, how Socrates' story ended: the Athenian authorities, unappreciative of having their authority questioned and ignorance revealed, determined that Socrates was corrupting the youth and sentenced him to death.

Two generations later, Aristotle (the student of Socrates' own student, Plato) adopted what may have been the first back-to-basics approach to education. In his own school, the Lyceum, he used repetitive practice to develop good habits, morality, discipline, and reasoning abilities in his students (Steutel & Spiecker, 2004). The school's curriculum consisted of practical knowledge such as mathematics, reading and writing, natural sciences, physical education, and the humanities—history, poetry, politics, and the like (Ornstein & Levine, 2008). Aristotle could, no doubt, boast that his curriculum supported worldly success—after all, his most famous student, Alexander the Great, had conquered most of the known world.

It would appear, then, that two of the arguably greatest minds of the ancient world were at odds with one another regarding how to teach the youth of Athens: Where Socrates preferred an open-ended approach to curriculum, one that *expanded* students' minds, teaching them to think deeply and develop a thirst for wisdom and knowledge, Aristotle believed that a more structured approach to curriculum was best—one that *molded* young minds and moral behavior through discipline and guided practice.

The question of which type of curriculum "works" best remains an open one, with debates raging from antiquity to modern times over exactly what knowledge we should impart to students.

What We Know and *Don't* Know from Education Research

It would be nice, of course, if there were some way to put the question to an empirical test—to use research to divine which knowledge and skills create the most successful, happiest people. However, there's really no way to do that. With something as large and ever-changing as a K–12 curriculum, it's difficult, if not impossible, to find a "smoking gun" in the annals of scientific research. To date, no rigorous, experimental-design studies have been conducted on K–12 curricula to determine exactly what scope-and-sequence students should follow from kindergarten through high school to succeed in college or the workplace.

Certainly, some curricular programs have been found to have a positive impact on student success. But studies of these programs are usually of a small grain size; they tend to report, for example, that a specific mathematics program has helped students perform better on a standardized measure of achievement during a limited period (e.g., two or three years).

Student Course-Taking Patterns: Algebra II a Necessary Rite of Passage?

Other studies have correlated certain course-taking patterns with college success. These studies tell us, for example, that students who successfully complete four years of high school English are more likely to demonstrate college-readiness skills on college entrance exams such as the ACT (ACT Inc., 2008). Studies also show that students who complete Algebra II are more than twice as likely to graduate from college compared to students with less mathematical preparation (U.S. Department of Education, 2008).

One problem with these findings, however, is that they offer little, if any, insight into exactly *which* knowledge and skills contained within those courses are most vital to students' later academic success. Moreover, because the studies are *correlational*, not *causal*, there's no way to know whether the knowledge gained, for example, from an Algebra II course is critical to college success, or whether the various dispositions, background knowledge, and external factors that contribute to students' enrolling and doing well in a higher-level mathematics courses are the *real* keys to their later academic achievement.

International Comparisons: The Effects of a "Mile-Wide, Inch-Deep" Curriculum

William Schmidt and colleagues compared the performance of students on the *Third International Mathematics and Science Study* (TIMSS), a test given regularly to a sampling of students at all grade levels in as many as 50 countries (the number of countries participating depends on the test). On most of these math and science tests, U.S. students tend to score near the top in the world in 4th grade but a little below average by the 8th grade. As Schmidt writes, "U.S. students did not start behind, they fell behind" (Schmidt, McKnight, Cogan, Jakwerth, & Houang, 1999).

Schmidt and his colleagues set out to determine what's happening to U.S. students in the black box between 4th and 8th grade. They considered, for example, whether U.S. students might be spending *less time* on mathematics and science than their foreign peers, receiving a different (presumably less rigorous) curriculum, or being taught with different (and presumably inferior) teaching methods.

In response to the first question, they found that, on average, U.S. students were actually spending *more* time on mathematics instruction than their international counterparts. Thus, they could confidently strike inadequate time devoted to math and science from their list of likely causes for the sagging achievement.

In terms of curriculum, though, they found a big difference between the United States and other countries. Specifically, they found that "U.S. mathematics and science curricula were largely unfocused ... and highly repetitive" (p. 27). They found, for example, that where U.S. mathematics textbooks tend to cover 32 topics at the 4th grade level and 38 in 8th grade, textbooks in other countries tend to cover 19 and 23 topics, respectively. Employing a phrase that has now become common in education parlance, the researchers found that U.S. mathematics and science curricula tend to be "a mile wide and an inch deep."

Schmidt and his colleagues also found that, perhaps as a result of the need to cover a plethora of topics, teachers in the United States used different teaching styles than their counterparts abroad—especially those in higher-performing countries. Specifically, the researchers gleaned from surveys of teachers from around the world that U.S. math classrooms tend to be "dominated by homework and seatwork" (p. 78). Students in the United States spend more time solving problems than writing equations and discussing them in class (as is more common in top-performing Japan). It would seem that grinding through 38 major math concepts in a single year—that's a little more than one per week—doesn't leave much time for the kind of higher-order thinking that's more common in Asian classrooms.

Schmidt and his colleagues speculated that something else may be at work in the United States. They found that despite the large number of topics U.S. teachers are supposed to cover, they actually (and somewhat ironically) appear to spend *more* time reviewing what students have learned and *less* time introducing new concepts than teachers in higher-performing countries. In mathematics classrooms, in particular, instead of treating math knowledge as an ever-evolving and expanding set of skills and strategies that students integrate to solve problems, math concepts appear to be regarded in the United States as discrete chunks of knowledge that students must acquire and hold in their heads. So instead of challenging students with increasingly complex problems that require an ever-evolving set of computational and analytical skills to solve, U.S. students are, instead, constantly quizzed and reviewed to make sure that none of their fine-grain knowledge has leaked out of their brains for want of use. We'll return to this observation later in the chapter.

School-Level Effects: Students Can't Learn What They Haven't Been Taught

We *do* know from research that Robert Marzano conducted several years ago at McREL that the school-level variable with the strongest apparent link to student success is "opportunity to learn"—that is, the extent to which a school (1) clearly articulates its curriculum, (2) monitors the extent to which teachers cover the curriculum, and (3) aligns its curriculum with assessments used to measure student achievement (Marzano, 2000). Of these three variables, the third—aligning curriculum to assessments—appears to have the strongest link with student achievement.

As Marzano noted, the effect size of the first two variables is equivalent to about a seven-percentage-point difference in student achievement. But when all three variables are combined, their effect size is on par with a 31-percentage-point difference in achievement. The not-so-surprising conclusion to be drawn from this finding is that students perform better on tests when they've been taught the content and skills on the test.

Answers to the "Big Questions" Still Elude Us

As interesting and useful as the above findings may be, they don't really answer "big picture" curriculum questions, such as "What knowledge and skills are most important for students to learn in order to be successful in life?" Certainly, many organizations have identified "college readiness" or "workplace readiness" standards. And a national effort has just been completed that identifies a "common core" of learning that students need to be successful in college and the workplace. Yet, because of the lack of rigorous scientific research in this area, these efforts, no matter how thoughtful and reasoned, still remain educated guesses as to what's most important for students to learn.

Finding the Touchstones for Curriculum: Two Narratives

To help identify what matters most when it comes to curricula, I offer a pair of modern narratives to illustrate two contrasting touchstones for curriculum design. At first blush, they may appear like the two roads that diverge in Robert Frost's "The Road Not Taken," offering very different paths for reform. One sees uniformly high standards for all students as the key to improving their life choices; the other views uniquely individualized or personalized learning pathways as the key to maximizing their potential. Current practice sometimes construes these approaches as mutually exclusive. However, they are not necessarily contradictory; indeed, they can be balanced as complementary principles. In short, unlike the choice made in the Frost poem to follow a single path and leave the other for another day, it is possible—even necessary—for educators to follow both paths simultaneously.

One Path: A High-Expectations Curriculum for All

On December 7, 1982, this headline appeared in the metro section of the *Los Angeles Times*:

> 14 STUDENTS RETAKE TEST AFTER SCORES ARE DISPUTED—
> PRINCIPAL CHARGES MINORITY BIAS.

The story, which reported that the Educational Testing Service, the company that contracts with the College Board to administer the tests, had accused students in a high school in East Los Angeles, California, of cheating on Advanced Placement (AP) tests, did not raise many eyebrows, as students have undoubtedly been cheating on tests since humans first touched carbon to papyrus. It likely would have passed mostly unnoticed had it not piqued the curiosity of a reporter in the Los Angeles bureau of the *Washington Post* (Mathews, 1988, p. 1).

Jay Mathews, recently returned to the United States after a long overseas stint in the China bureau of the *Post*, was intrigued by a simple factoid at the heart of the incident. He asked himself, How did a place like Garfield High School, in a high-poverty, gang-infested neighborhood, "find eighteen students willing to take the AP calculus test at all?" (p. 1).

Mathews dug deeper and discovered that the secret to the students' success was not cheating; rather, it was a singularly inspired and talented teacher: Jaime Escalante. Mathews observed Escalante's classroom for many months, watching him blend unrelenting high expectations and tough love to transform his students into true college-bound scholars. Eventually, Escalante was vindicated after 12 of his students retook the test and passed it again. Mathews recorded his observations in the book *Escalante: The Best Teacher in America*, which inspired the 1988 film *Stand and Deliver*.

But the story did not end there. Years later, while researching some of the nation's best high schools, Mathews was stunned to find one such school, Mamaroneck High School in Westchester County, New York, barring students from taking AP courses. He was outraged. Here was Mamaroneck, a school regarded as one of the best in the United States, denying students access to courses that would give them a significant leg up on college success. On the other hand, Garfield, which was dramatically changing the odds for many of its low-income students, was viewed by many in L.A. as a lousy school because of its low overall scores on the state test.

The Challenge Index

At the time that Mathews encountered Mamaroneck, he was covering Wall Street, a land ruled by indexes: the Dow Jones, the S&P 500, the NASDAQ. He decided to create his own index to help show "why Garfield, in a neighborhood full of auto-body shops and fast-food joints, was at least as good a school as Mamaroneck, in a town of mansions and country clubs" (Mathews, 2007). The result was the Challenge Index, which the *Washington Post* and *Newsweek* now use every year to identify and rank the best high schools in the United States. The formula for the index is simple:

$$\frac{\text{\# of AP / International Baccalaureate (IB) tests taken by all students in a school}}{\text{\# number of graduating seniors}}$$

The Challenge Index is not without its critics, many of whom argue that it fails to take into account dropout rates or student success on the AP tests. Indeed, a growing number of schools have begun to boycott the index altogether, refusing to send data to *Newsweek* and the *Post* (Mathews, 2008a). Mathews acknowledges that the index is a narrow measure of school performance but insists that it is narrow by design—to highlight an important and often-overlooked metric of how well schools are preparing average students for success in college. And, by many counts, this outcome—preparing more students for college—may be the biggest challenge facing our nation's schools.

Over the past few decades, the percentage of citizens with college degrees has increased only slightly in the United States, while it's steadily increased in other countries. Moreover, in the United States, college graduation rates for some minority groups appear to be dwindling, for the first time in our nation's history (American Council on Education, 2008). According to statistics from the Manhattan Institute, only 32 percent of all students in the United States leave high school qualified to attend four-year colleges. The percentages are even lower for black and Hispanic students, with 20 and 16 percent, respectively, leaving high school college-ready. After comparing these data with college completion rates, researchers concluded that poor preparation for college, and not "inadequate financial aid or affirmative action policies," is the main reason for minority underrepresentation on college campuses (Greene & Foster, 2003, p. 2).

College Prep "Shock Treatment"

In response to these and other data, a growing number of schools and districts appear to be adopting the slogan "College preparation for all" and throwing open the doors of their AP classes: According to the College Board, the company that creates the AP tests, enrollment in AP courses nationwide rose 50 percent from 2004 to 2009 (College Board, 2009). However, the percentage of high school graduates actually passing an AP exam rose by only 3.2 percent during the same period (College Board, 2010).

Some districts have gone so far as to place *all* students in AP or IB classes, even those otherwise enrolled in remedial courses (Sanders & Palka, 2009). In a 2009 article, *Newsweek* magazine likened these efforts to channel every student into rigorous college-preparatory courses as a kind of "academic shock treatment." The hope is that making students take tough classes will, like spending a week in the gym with a personal trainer, whip them into academic shape, forcing them to develop the cognitive muscles they need for college success.

Whether this form of academic "tough love" really works, though, remains an open question. For starters, taking an AP class is no guarantee of passing the AP exam. For example, a reporter in Duval County, Florida, discovered that while AP enrollment tripled in the county, only 23 percent of AP exams taken were passed, despite more than 80 percent of students receiving Cs or better in the classes that were supposed to be preparing them for success on the exams. In the county's four lowest-performing high schools, only 6 percent of the AP exams taken received passing scores (Sanders & Palka, 2009).

Nor does simply *taking* AP classes appear to contribute to college success. Saul Geiser and his colleagues at the University of California–Berkeley examined the records of more than 80,000 students in the University of California system and determined that while *passing* the AP exam *does* correlate with student success in college, simply taking the courses "bears little or no relationship to students' later performance in college" (Geiser & Santelices, 2004, p. 18). In a 2009 editorial in *The New York Times*, Geiser concluded that "The key is not simply taking AP, but mastering the material" (Geiser, 2009).

Jay Mathews himself altered the Challenge Index after noticing an increase in the number of schools with big spikes in AP enrollment yet dismal passing rates on the tests. "The minute I saw that Coolidge High School in [Washington, D.C.] had given a startling 750 Advanced Placement tests last May, and that only 2 percent of those exams had received passing scores, I knew I was in trouble," he wrote on his blog in December 2008 (Mathews, 2008b). With 750 tests taken and 137 graduating seniors, Coolidge's Challenge Index rating shot to 5.474, making it the top school in the D.C. metro area—even higher than H-B Woodlawn in Arlington, Virginia, where 59 percent of students had passed their exams.

Rather than kick Coolidge and schools like it off the *Newsweek* list, Mathews created a new "Catching Up" category for schools with 10 percent or lower passing rates on AP exams. Still a staunch believer in the need to shine a bright light on schools that are providing more kids with access to college-preparatory coursework, Mathews applauded the efforts of Coolidge's principal, who said he was using the AP tests—which are scored by outside experts and, therefore, cannot be dumbed down—to give kids in low-income neighborhoods "the icy blast of real college standards."

Many educators insist that offering AP classes to average and below-average students is an important first step. Over time, as teachers become more comfortable teaching the curriculum and students come to understand what is expected of them, passing rates should rise. Fearing the slippery slope of lowering expectations, the "shock treatment" proponents remain convinced that providing all students with AP courses is better than nothing at all.

A Path Less Traveled: Personalized Curriculum

At nearly the same time that Mathews was reporting the story of Jaime Escalante in East L.A., a similar tale of an unorthodox educator caught in the crosshairs of the establishment was unfolding in the opposite corner of the country. In the small New England town of Winchester, New Hampshire, a principal with a radical vision for transforming Thayer High School had split the town in two.

A local reporter from the Keene *Sentinel*, Susan Kammeraad-Campbell, stumbled across the story when she arrived one evening in 1985 at a meeting of the Winchester school board—ordinarily a dreadfully dull assignment for a reporter (Kammeraad-Campbell, 1990). As she drove up to the elementary school where the meeting was being held, though, she noticed something odd: The parking lot was full. Inside the packed school library, she witnessed a contentious dispute among two sharply polarized factions.

The topic of debate was the board's behind-closed-doors decision to remove Thayer from Theodore Sizer's Coalition of Essential Schools. Between 1979 and 1984, Sizer, a professor of education at Brown University, had conducted a major study of U.S. secondary schools and concluded that the "unintentional mindlessness" of large, anonymous "shopping mall" schools "virtually guarantees inadequate work from the students" (Sizer, 1992a, p. vii). Through his series of *Horace* books, Sizer had taken on the status quo of U.S. education. The books described the saga of Horace Smith, a fictional high school English teacher. Horace's frustration was with the multiple compromises that high schools force teachers to make each day—for example, teaching a curriculum that helps students jump through the hoops needed to get into college but does little to develop their critical-thinking skills or forcing teachers to stand in front of more students than one teacher can possibly get to know, let alone mentor. These compromises lead Horace to call for a dramatic restructuring of his school.

Using Horace as his avatar, Sizer proposed that high school students demonstrate their learning through "exhibitions"—cross-curricular opportunities for students to delve deeply into content, pursue their own interests, and engage in real-world learning (see sidebar for examples). One of Sizer's key ideas (and the origin for the name of his coalition) is that schools should first identify what is *essential* for students to know and then work from there to determine how they should learn it. As he wrote in *Horace's School*, "We must make choices about what is essential and encourage all students' appropriate and sustained involvement with this most important material" (1992b, p. 147). The key challenge of schools, wrote Sizer, was to hold high expectations for students, yet do so in a way that respected students' individual interests. Or as he put it, "The task [of school reform] is the creation of a loose system that has rigor" (p. 115).

Through his Coalition of Essential Schools, which at its peak included 1,000 schools nationwide, Sizer sought to create a more personal, democratic, and engaging form of schooling based on the following "five imperatives" for better schools:

> 1) Give room to teachers and students to work and learn in their own appropriate ways, 2) Insist that students clearly exhibit mastery of their work, 3) Get the

A Closer Look: Student "Exhibitions" from *Horace's School*

In *Horace's School*, Ted Sizer offers several examples of student "exhibitions"—projects designed to develop high school students' critical-thinking skills and "be taken seriously" while allowing "students to pursue areas of their own interest and use multiple media."

Here are two examples:

- "Assemble from metal pipes a wind instrument. Write a piece of music that uses it and perform this piece for us. Present to us design drawings for the instrument and be prepared to explain precisely how it works" (p. 118).

- "Select one of the following emotions: fear, envy, courage, hunger, longing, joy, anger, greed, jealousy. In an essay, define the emotion you choose, drawing on your own and others' experience. Then render a similar definition using in turn at least three of the following forms of expression: a written language other than English; a piece of drawing, painting, or sculpture; photographs, a video, or film; a musical composition; a short story or play; pantomime; a dance" (p. 23).

Source: From *Horace's School: Redesigning the American High School*, by T. Sizer, 1992, New York: Houghton Mifflin Company.

incentives right, for students and for teachers, 4) Focus the students' work on the use of their minds, 5) Keep the structure simple and thus flexible. (Sizer, 1992b, p. 214)

However, when Kammeraad-Campbell dug deeper into the tumult at the Winchester school board meeting, she discovered that the real issue in the community was not so much with Ted Sizer or the Coalition of Essential Schools, but rather with the principal of Thayer High School, Sheldon "Doc" Dennis Littky, who had taken Sizer's ideas to heart and was zealously working to implement them. During Littky's tenure as principal between 1981 and 1984, the school's dropout rate had fallen from 20 to 1 percent, and the number of students enrolling in college had climbed from 10 to 55 percent (Littky & Grabelle, 2004). Those accomplishments might have made Littky the most popular man in town had his methods not seemed so unorthodox to the local community.

Littky was convinced that the way to keep students in school was to get them *outside* of school, to see how learning applied to the real world. He worked with local businesses to create internship programs for students. He changed school hours so teachers had time to hold conferences with individual students, essentially creating individual learning plans for each student.

An avid disciple of Sizer, Littky espoused a "less is more" approach to learning. Believing that curriculum should be designed to foster mastery, not simply coverage, he extended class periods for his "outdoor" science teacher so that students could spend more time studying nature in the woods that surround Winchester. The culmination of his "less is more" approach to curricula was the creation of a multidisciplinary program called Dovetail, during which students engaged in such projects as building the school's new environmental studies center and conducting a detailed historical survey of the neighboring town of Richmond.

Despite the school's successes and increasing attention from regional and national media, a vocal group of critics in Winchester began to lobby the school board to remove Littky from his position. Many of those seeking his ouster feared that his iconoclastic, nonauthoritarian approach—embodied by casual attire and "mountain man" beard—ran counter to what students needed: structure and respect for authority. For example, when the Keene *Sentinel* ran a front-page photo of Thayer students watching television coverage of the *Challenger* disaster, which took the life of Christa McAuliffe (a teacher from nearby Concord), the newspaper received an angry letter from a reader who was outraged because some students in the photo were shown wearing baseball caps inside the school.

Others were scandalized when Littky allowed a pregnant teen to conduct, as a school project, a community survey on teenage pregnancy. One local business owner refused to let her give the survey on his store premises. (Incidentally, the student, who had been on the verge of dropping out after becoming pregnant, went on to become an honor student and her class president.)

By March 1986, a few months after the fiery board meeting, Littky's critics prevailed, and the Winchester school board fired him. Shortly after his termination, his photo appeared on the cover of the *New England Monthly* above the caption, "He's the Best Educator in New England. And He's Just Been Fired" (Goldberg, 1990).

Littky fought what he viewed as a wrongful dismissal. After a heated 18-month battle, he was finally reinstated. His struggles became the subject of the book *Doc: The Story of Dennis Littky and His Fight for a Better School* by Kammeraad-Campbell and also of the ABC made-for-TV movie *A Town Torn Apart*. After his vindication, Littky stayed on at Thayer for several more years, refining his radical approach to education. Eventually, he took his vision to Providence, Rhode Island, where he started the Metropolitan Regional Career and Technical Center (known as the Met Center) in 1996. Today, Littky's organization, Big Picture Learning, which is supported by such philanthropies as the Bill and Melinda Gates Foundation, includes a network of more than 60 schools nationwide. Students in Big Picture schools prepare themselves for college not necessarily by spending more time in AP classrooms but by getting out into the world, learning through internships and adult mentors, and demonstrating their learning through quarterly portfolio assessments known as "exhibitions" (a term borrowed from Sizer) (Littky & Grabelle, 2004). It's an approach Littky calls "treating everyone alike differently." As Littky notes,

> From the way we design curricula and standards to the way we design schools, we must think of the individual and what he or she needs and wants from education. I cannot state this more strongly: This is the only way schools will really work and the only way every kid will be offered the education he or she deserves. (p. 73)

A Closer Look: Student Projects in Big Picture Learning Schools

In Big Picture Learning schools, high school students spend two days each week working on "internships," typically work outside of school guided by a trained adult mentor. Here are two examples of these projects:

- A 9th grader calculated the profit margin at a boutique where she was working.

- Another 9th grader, after his uncle was shot and killed in a bar and the assailant was never identified, wrote and lobbied his state legislature to pass a law requiring security cameras to be placed in every bar.

Source: From "Time Goes By, Everything Looks the Same," by D. Littky, 2010, *Interactions*. Retrieved September 13, 2010, from http://www.bigpicture.org/2010/07/time-goes-by-everything-looks-the-same/.

Littky blames the one-size-fits-all approach common in many high schools for students' falling through the cracks and dropping out. "No matter how hard schools try," he writes, "a one-size-fits-all approach to education will always be hit or miss" (p. 74). He insists there cannot be a uniform curriculum for every student in the country or even for every student in a single classroom. "Force-feeding kids a rigidly defined body of knowledge," he notes, "is in total opposition to what we know about learning" (p. 75).

Motivation 3.0 in the Classroom

The underlying power of Littky's personalized approach to learning may lie in what author Daniel Pink calls "motivation 3.0"—that is, using autonomy and mastery experiences to tap into students' natural curiosity and intrinsic motivation to learn (Pink, 2010, p. 77).

The current reality, however, is that in many classrooms and schools, students often have little autonomy or control over their own learning, which can leave them unmotivated or even resistant to learning. Teachers often respond to students' listlessness by turning to what Pink describes as the old version of motivation, "motivation 2.0"—namely, rewards and punishments. To get kids to do what they're "supposed" to do, many teachers resort to giving out candy for good performance or cancelling recess when students don't turn in their homework. The net effect of these carrot-and-stick approaches is that over time, students come to view learning not as something they should intrinsically *want* to do, but rather as something they *must* do if they want candy or to go to the playground. Moreover, as with drugs, the effect of these incentives tends to diminish over time, creating the need for ever-increasing doses of rewards and punishments.

The Power of Choices

Admittedly, for teachers who feel that no amount of cajoling, goading, or browbeating will motivate their students to learn, it may seem counterintuitive, if not a bit foolish, to give reluctant students more freedom and expect them to learn more. Yet that's exactly what a team of researchers led by Erika Patall found when they conducted a meta-analysis of research on student choice and achievement: a strong link between giving students choices about their learning and intrinsic motivation, task performance, and willingness to assume challenging tasks (Patall, Cooper, & Robinson, 2008).

It's important to note that these same researchers also found diminishing returns for *how many* choices teachers give their students: in particular, offering *more than five* options appears to have less benefit for learning than offering just three to five options. When presented with too many choices, students, especially novice learners, can become overwhelmed or expend too much mental energy in making the choice instead of actually doing the work. Thus, Patall and her colleagues concluded that with student choice, "too much of a good thing may not be very good at all" (p. 298).

Bear in mind, too, that the choices offered don't have to be instructionally relevant. Indeed, Patall and her colleagues concluded that *instructionally irrelevant* choices—for example, choosing which colors to learn how to pronounce in a foreign language—had the greatest positive effect on intrinsic motivation. The point here is that a little bit of latitude can go a long way—as any parent of a toddler knows. There's probably not a three-year-old alive who likes being informed that it's bedtime, but most parents know that giving a child a simple (and for parents, irrelevant) choice in her bedtime routine (e.g., "Do you want to wear your Dora the Explorer or Ariel

Try This: Tap "Motivation 3.0" by Giving Students Choices

Teachers often lack the ability to create multiple curricular pathways for students but can still control how they *deliver* curricula to students. One simple approach to personalizing classroom experiences for students is to give them some controlled choices.

Here are a few examples of the ways in which teachers can use choices to give students some control over their own learning, while keeping curriculum aligned with standards and high expectations:

- Give science students the choice of two or three preselected readings that illustrate the same concept (e.g., the interdependence of ecosystems).

- Let middle school language arts students choose from a list of young adult novels, analyzing each for the same elements, such as plot structure, themes, character development, and author's worldview.

- Give elementary students a list of assignments to complete (e.g., spelling words, silent reading, grammar assignments) but let them choose the order in which to complete them.

- Provide young students with simple (even instructionally irrelevant) choices, such as what color pencils or paper to use for an assignment.

the Mermaid pajamas?") can melt resistance and send her hurrying off to begin her nighttime ritual.

As children grow older, though, they become more sophisticated and require more relevant choices to feed their intrinsic motivation. Limiting student choices (for example, forcing them to enroll in an AP course whether or not they have any desire to be there) would appear to fly in the face of what we know about intrinsic motivation. As Daniel Pink notes, "All kids start out as curious, self-directed" learners, yet when it comes to motivating students to learn, "there's a mismatch between what science knows and schools do" (2010, p. 174). By giving students fewer choices, not more, and offering them "if-then" extrinsic rewards for performance (for example, doling out iPods and pizza parties for good grades), many schools are systematically stamping out students' natural curiosity and bent for mastery learning.

On the other hand, providing students with meaningful choices—choices that, no matter what option they select, will prepare them for life success—can tap the powerful drive that exists in each of us to challenge ourselves and develop mastery in areas that interest us. And, as we'll see in a moment, that's exactly what a growing number of successful high school programs, many of them inspired by Littky himself, are doing.

Putting the Touchstones to the Test

As in the previous chapter, let's put to the test these two seemingly paradoxical touchstones of curriculum—that is, that on the one hand, it should be *standardized* to ensure it provides students with the rigorous preparation they need to succeed in life, while on the other hand, it should be *personalized* to tap students' intrinsic motivation for engaging in mastery learning. If these really are the keys to curriculum, we should expect to see them both at work in effective schools.

Lessons from the *It's Being Done* Schools

Karin Chenoweth, a longtime education reporter for the *Washington Post* who now writes for the Education Trust organization, has profiled two dozen beat-the-odds schools in her books *It's Being Done: Academic Success in Unexpected Schools* (2007) and *How It's Being Done: Urgent Lessons from*

Unexpected Schools (2009). A recurring theme among the success stories she recounts may contradict what some misty-eyed (or perhaps it's "Dewey-eyed") educators have come to believe about education: that students simply need the opportunity to explore their environments and nurture their natural talents under the watchful eye of a supportive, caring teacher. The stories of these schools may also run counter to the narrative that others might wish to hear: that turnaround schools have followed a sort of "bootstraps" story line, finding a way despite impossible odds through their own ingenuity and hard work to help students succeed.

Many Turnaround Schools Adopt "Off-the-Shelf" Curricula

The reality appears to be that many beat-the-odds schools (especially at the elementary level) have actually adopted prepackaged, "off-the-shelf" curricular programs, such as America's Choice, Success for All, Everyday Math, Open Court, and Core Knowledge. These programs typically arrive at a school's doorstep complete with student readers, lesson plans for teachers, and consultants who train teachers in how to use the materials.

An oft-heard complaint from educators about these programs is that they are overly scripted or limit teachers' ability to be creative or respond to student needs. However, Chenoweth found that leaders and teachers in the *It's Being Done* schools were almost uniformly positive about these programs. For them, it seems that adopting "off-the-shelf" curricula served a handful of key purposes.

For starters, the programs helped schools raise their expectations for students practically overnight. For example, after adopting the Core Knowledge curriculum (among other changes in the school), Capitol View Elementary School in Atlanta, Georgia, can now boast that 100 percent of the school's high-poverty 5th graders are meeting or exceeding state reading standards. Trennis Harvey, the school's instruction specialist, credited the Core Knowledge curriculum with forcing the school to raise the bar for students by proving that, as Harvey put it, "kids will meet the standards you expect of them" (Chenoweth, 2007, p. 166).

Implementing a prepackaged program also appears to have helped schools ensure greater continuity of curriculum, especially in environments that are often plagued with high teacher turnover. Without a clearly defined curriculum, every new teacher who steps into a school is likely to create his or her own curriculum and set his or her own expectations for learning. As a result, some classrooms and lessons offer a challenging curriculum, but many others do not.

A final point to consider is that low-performing schools often have many novice teachers, who struggle mightily in their first couple of years on the job to figure out how to manage classroom behavior, learn students' names, understand the routines of the schools, grade papers and quizzes, track student progress, *and* wrap their heads around the curriculum in order to create engaging lesson plans. Leaders in the turnaround schools that Chenoweth profiled reported that giving teachers a well-defined curriculum let them worry less about *what* to teach and more about *how* to teach it.

A Personal Story

Permit me to offer a personal aside. Two months into my first year of teaching high school, an odd smell emanating from the corner of my classroom sent me poking around in some previously unexplored filing cabinets. Before long, I made an appalling discovery: a dead mouse lay in the bottom drawer of one cabinet. However, in that same drawer, I stumbled across nearly an entire year's worth of lesson plans left behind by the teacher who had previously occupied my room and taught my classes. Her lessons were *immaculate*, complete with learning objectives, teaching strategies, and even prompts to use when checking for student understanding. For an overwhelmed first-year teacher, it was the sort of discovery that made me feel as if clouds had parted and a chorus of angels had begun singing in the heavens.

Many first-year teachers, of course, don't have the benefit of a dead mouse leading them to a treasure trove of lesson plans. Instead, they are left to design their own curricula, often learning from students along the way that they're teaching something that has already been taught in a previous year, or divining from blank stares that their students don't yet have the background knowledge they need to comprehend what's being taught.

Taking Lesson Planning Off New Teachers' Plates

I remember feeling a bit ashamed and guilt-ridden about using another teacher's lesson plans—as if I were somehow shirking my duties or plagiarizing someone else's work. What the high-performing schools Chenoweth profiled did is remove that guilt and anxiety for teachers by simply *telling them* what to teach, letting them know that they don't have to figure it all out by themselves. Indeed, some of them, such as the Roxbury Prep Charter Academy, went a step further, actually compiling and *giving* teachers three-ring binders full of well-designed lesson plans at the beginning of the year. Similarly, at Lockhart Junior High School in Lockhart, Texas, new teachers were handed an entire year's worth of lesson plans when they walked in the door.

Far from feeling that their creativity or professionalism had been compromised (or guilty about not planning their own lessons), the teachers at these schools welcomed the support and the ability to focus their energies on instruction and classroom management. "It was overwhelming my first year," one Lockhart teacher told Chenoweth. "There was just a lot to keep up with and keep track of." Being able to strike lesson planning from her list of first-year worries removed a few creases from her brow and made her feel "like I had support" (Chenoweth, 2009, p. 101).

Reflections on "Off-the-Shelf" Curricula

At first blush, these stories all appear to reinforce the value of imposing a rigid, one-size-fits-all approach to curricula. To some extent, perhaps they do. Many struggling schools, which usually face the need to get their curricular house in order quickly, appear to benefit from adopting an outside curriculum. For a low-performing school facing a multitude of challenges, not the least of which likely is a revolving door of inexperienced teachers, adopting an outside curriculum can help to quickly address the need to ensure that students are being appropriately challenged.

However, not every school that attempts to adopt an outside curriculum is successful, for reasons we'll explore in more depth in Chapter 5. (Indeed, one school Chenoweth profiled had been *unsuccessfully* using Success for All for a number of years—in part, because a previous instructional coach had turned the program into a cudgel with which to beat teachers with "nasty grams" and criticisms of their failing to follow the program to a T, rather than as a platform to improve their instruction [Chenoweth, 2009, p. 85].)

It's also worth pointing out that adopting an outside, off-the-shelf curriculum is not the *only* path to success for schools. Indeed, many beat-the-odds schools Chenoweth profiled had developed their own curricula, engaging in time-consuming (yet ultimately rewarding) curriculum mapping processes. Teachers in those schools worked together to identify what they would teach to students at each level—down to exacting details such as whether alliteration should be taught in the 3rd or 4th grade. When it works well, a curriculum mapping and alignment process can help schools begin to shape a new, more collaborative and professional culture in their school. Of course, the success of such efforts likely depends on having some critical mass of experienced teachers in the school who are willing and able to undergo the process of designing a schoolwide curriculum.

Getting Away from a "Burger King" Model of Curriculum

The bottom line, though, is that *all* of the high-performing schools Chenoweth profiled tell a similar story—of working hard to get their curriculum in order, to ensure they set high expectations for students, and to deliver curriculum in a consistent way from classroom to classroom. While the particulars and plotlines of their success stories vary, each school appears to have arrived at the same end point: a curriculum tightly aligned with high standards and a way to ensure that everyone in the school was teaching it.

In short, the schools made certain that what gets taught in the classroom is not left to guesswork or the whims of individual teachers—what Robert Marzano refers to as creating a "guaranteed and viable curriculum" (Marzano, 2003, p. 22). Or as the chief academic officer at M. Hall Stanton Elementary School, a high-performing school in Philadelphia, told Chenoweth, one key to his school's success was getting away from the "Burger King" model of curriculum—where teachers "got to have it their way" (Chenoweth, 2007, p. 128).

When left to their own devices, it's unlikely that teachers will align curriculum in their schools, *even if* every teacher in the school holds high expectations for students and designs rigorous curricula and lesson plans. As a result, students will wind up repeating some material, and other important learning may fall through the cracks. The end result may be like that of many people in a rowboat all pulling furiously on their oars, yet rowing in different directions and leaving the boat spinning in circles.

Making Learning Meaningful: An Antidote to the Dropout Crisis

To be clear: simply providing more challenging content can, by itself, motivate students. As noted in the last chapter, human beings are natural-born problem solvers. We find challenging problems more interesting than easy ones; we are more drawn to put together a 200-piece jigsaw puzzle than a two-piece one. The same thing can be said for students. Indeed, according to the Gates Foundation–funded *Silent Epidemic* report, a 2006 survey of students who had dropped out of school, fully two-thirds of these students said they would have worked harder if more had been expected of them (Bridgeland, Diulio, & Morison, 2006). Not being challenged in school led to boredom, which in turn led to students skipping class and eventually dropping out of school.

In many respects, then, challenging students is obviously a key part of the student motivation equation. However, it does not appear to be the whole equation.

The authors of the *Silent Epidemic* report found that in addition to not being challenged, another key reason students dropped out was being unable to connect what they were learning with the real world. Indeed, almost half (47 percent) of the high school dropouts surveyed said that they quit school because the "classes were not interesting." As one student remarked, "They make you take classes in school that you're never going to use in life" (p. 4). Fully 81 percent of dropouts said that providing "opportunities for real-world learning (internships, service learning, etc.) to make classroom[s] more relevant" would have increased their chances of staying in school (p. 13).

Personalizing Learning in High School

For more than two decades, the Southern Region Education Board (SREB) has been testing, refining, and advocating for a personalized approach to education in hundreds of high schools nationwide through its High Schools that Work network of schools. The model focuses on providing every student with a rigorous foundation in academic preparation, high-quality career and technical education, and ongoing career guidance from mentors. SREB researchers have concluded that such a personalized approach is the best way for high schools to raise both standards and graduation rates. For example, after examining 13 successful Georgia high schools where test scores

A Closer Look: California Partnership Academies

For more than two decades, California Partnership Academies have provided at-risk high school students with rigorous academic preparation that focuses on career themes, such as health sciences, architecture, and finance.

A 2007 study of 12,000 students enrolled in 287 career academies found that these students were more likely than their nonacademy peers to pass the state's high school exit exams as sophomores, graduate from high school, and take college-preparatory coursework. The benefits of attending a career academy appeared to be most pronounced for at-risk students. For example, 71 percent of black sophomores enrolled in career academies passed the math portion of the California high school exit exam, compared with just 55 percent of all black high school sophomores in the state.

Source: From *A Profile of the California Partnership Academies, 2004–2005,* by D. Bradby, A. Malloy, T. Hanna, and C. Dayton, March 2007, Berkeley, CA: California Center for College and Career.

and student graduation rates were *both* rising, SREB concluded that the key to success for these schools was their twofold effort to both raise standards and personalize learning for students:

> These most-improved schools were not just about rigor; they were about students seeing a purpose in what they were being asked to learn. Leaders from these schools expressed a belief that high demand/high quality career/technical programs help students link what they learn in the academic classroom to something that matters to them personally. School leaders expressed the opinion that quality career/technical studies played a role in keeping students in school. (Southern Region Education Board, 2009b, p. 7)

A growing number of career academies are also offering students such real-world learning opportunities. To date, more than 2,500 academies exist nationwide, often as schools within schools. Typically, they offer a small group of students (around 30–60 per grade) both academic and career preparation around career themes such as health care, finance, business, engineering, media, and so on. A study of the outcomes of career academies on the lives of nearly 1,500 students from nine urban high schools found that, eight years after graduating, students who had gone through the career academies were earning 11 percent more (or $216 more per month) than their matched peers who had not gone through the academies. The effects were particularly pronounced for young males (approximately 85 percent of whom were minority); they were earning $312 more per month than their nonacademy peers (Kemple with Willner, 2008).

Taking the Path Less Traveled

In the November 2009 report *Ready for Tomorrow: Six Proven Ideas to Graduate and Prepare More Students for College and 21st-Century Careers*, SREB calls for school systems to create multiple pathways and "pave each pathway with a rigorous academic foundation and with rich, authentic learning drawn from a career field of particular interest to the student" (Southern Region Education Board, 2009b, p. v).

The SREB authors acknowledge that creating such a system is no small feat. Offering multiple pathways requires building new systems to monitor student progress, rethinking transportation, educating parents and students on the different pathways, developing staff expertise, and confronting, as Littky discovered, entrenched ideas about how schooling ought to be done. Nonetheless, SREB asserts that through its High Schools that Work initiative, it "has demonstrated—beyond any doubt—that when high school leaders and teachers nurture the distinctive interests and talents of all groups of students, they can help more students stay in school and find the motivation to prepare for college, careers or for both" (p. v).

The Big Apple's "Small Schools of Choice"

In 2002, New York City closed 23 of its most dysfunctional high schools and opened, in their place, 123 "small schools of choice." These relatively small high schools (enrolling about 100 students per grade) were designed to serve the district's most disadvantaged students by letting them select from a variety of career-themed options, such as business, hospitality and tourism, writing, science and the environment, and law. Before opening, the district required each small school to demonstrate that it would demand high levels of academic rigor by aligning its curricula to New York state standards or college-ready standards that exceeded that state's standards. In addition, they had show how

---

A Closer Look: Combining Academic and Career Preparation in High Schools that Work

Many trailblazing schools and districts are showing that integrating high standards with personalized instruction *can* be done.

One example is the Thornton Township High School in Harvey, Illinois, a member of the Southern Region Education Board's High Schools that Work network. The suburban school of 2,400 in south Chicago, which enrolls a 91 percent black population, created three new career-preparation "houses" in the areas of Arts and Communication; Business, Engineering, Natural Resources and Technology; and Health and Human Services.

In their sophomore year, students enroll in these "houses of excellence that provide majors and course concentrations blended with high-level college-prep studies." Since these houses were introduced three years ago, mathematics scores on the statewide assessment have shot up 23.5 percentage points, and reading scores have gone up by 8.6 percent.

Source: From *Combining Academic and Technical Studies to Prepare Students for College and Careers* (p. 6), by Southern Region Education Board, 2009, Atlanta, GA: SREB.

they would provide "personalization" for students, creating, for example, "advisory" structures (not unlike those of the Big Picture Learning schools) in which adult teachers would be paired with students to promote strong teacher–student relationships. Finally, the district required the new schools to develop partnerships with business and community groups to give students opportunities to learn real-world skills *outside* the classroom and bring more real-world learning *inside* the classroom.

In 2010, the research firm MDRC released results from a large, rigorous study of the program. It reported that students in the small schools had higher graduation rates than did students in a control group, most of whom remained in large, comprehensive high schools. While students in both groups were similar in terms of ethnicity and socioeconomic background (more than 90 percent minority and more than 80 percent high-poverty), those who enrolled in the small schools of choice demonstrated immediate benefits: by the end of the 9th grade, 69.4 percent of them were on track to graduate versus 58.3 percent of their peers at large, comprehensive high schools. By the end of four years of school, 68.7 percent of students in the small schools had graduated versus 61.9 percent of students in the large schools (Bloom, Thompson, & Unterman with Herlihy & Payne, 2010).

Although a 6.8 percent advantage in the small schools' graduation rates may not seem significant, the MDRC researchers note that it's equivalent to one-third of the graduation gap between white and black students. Moreover, because New York's small schools initiative was a large intervention, there's likely a great deal of variation among the small schools, with some likely providing much greater benefits for students than others. Over time, as these higher-performing schools are identified and emulated and the lower-performing ones are weeded out, the benefits of the small schools of choice may become even more pronounced.

The key takeaway from these findings, the researchers caution, is not simply that *small* schools are better. Rather, it's that the *personalized* learning environments, "where students had a better chance of being known and noticed, and teachers had a better chance of knowing enough about their charges to provide appropriate academic and socioemotional supports," are better (pp. 58–59).

Multiple Pathways in Mapleton

Another example of a district-level effort to create multiple pathways is occurring in Mapleton, Colorado, an urban-fringe district just north of Denver, which serves approximately 6,000 mostly Hispanic and low-income students. In 2001, the district, which had struggled to increase graduation rates for students, replaced its comprehensive high school with seven separate college-preparatory high schools (some housed as schools within the original high schools). The programs range from an international leadership academy (featuring an IB curriculum) to an expeditionary learning-based school of the arts, with many options in between. Mapleton has also restructured its elementary and middle schools, enabling a similar range of options for younger students. While still new, anecdotal evidence suggests the approach may be having a positive impact on students. For example, 100 percent of students at the MESA school, one of the district's high schools, and 90 percent of seniors in Mapleton High were accepted to college, earning $2.6 million in scholarships (Centers, 2008). In 2010, state test results revealed that while students in the high-poverty district are still scoring well below the state average, they have begun to demonstrate some gains in learning—up three points overall in reading and two points in mathematics over the previous year—bucking the overall statewide trend of flat achievement scores (Meyer, 2010).

Moving Beyond Grade-Level Groupings in Alaska

Another example of integrating a standards-based approach with personalized learning comes from the Chugach School District in Alaska. In the late 1990s, Chugach became famous for jettisoning grade levels in favor of providing separate learning pathways for all students.

Web Resources for Creating Multiple Pathways

Big Picture Learning (http://www.bigpicture.org)

The Big Picture Learning website provides video examples, podcasts, white papers, articles, and books all related to creating multiple-pathway curricula for students.

Career Academy Support Network (http://casn.berkeley.edu)

Located at the University of California–Berkeley, the Career Academy Support Network website offers research reports on the career academies model, implementation guides and articles, and an online library of career-themed curricula for high school students.

Coalition of Essential Schools (http://www.essentialschools.org)

The Coalition of Essential Schools website provides free resources related to personalizing learning, including tools for creating interdisciplinary programs and personalized learning opportunities for students.

ConnectED (http://www.connectedcalifornia.org)

This site, from the California Center for College and Career, provides research and resources, including sample career-themed curricular pathways, designed to help schools and districts adopt a multiple-pathways approach.

Continued on next page ❯

Web Resources for Creating Multiple Pathways (continued)

Edutopia (http://www.edutopia .org)

Created by the George Lucas Educational Foundation, the Edutopia site provides teacher resources for project-based learning, video examples of personalized learning in schools, and a collection of resources related to merging career and college preparation.

Reinventing Schools Coalition (http://www.reinventingschools .org)

The Reinventing Schools Coalition, founded by former Chugach superintendent Richard DeLorenzo, provides information on its website about its model as well as videos that show what its personalized model of learning looks like in classrooms and schools.

Southern Region Education Board (http://www.sreb.org)

Located one click off its homepage, SREB's High Schools that Work site provides resources, research, and services that support integrating career preparation into high schools.

Students in the high-poverty district spread over 200 square miles are allowed and encouraged to progress at their own rate of learning, which more often than not is an accelerated pace. In other words, instead of an entire class moving forward at the same plodding rate, students are allowed to shoot ahead in the curriculum once they demonstrate competency at a particular developmental level.

Letting students accelerate through the curriculum appears to be one of the most powerful practices available to educators. Of 138 influences on student achievement that John Hattie examined in his survey of research, he found that accelerated learning ranked *fifth* with a whopping effect size of $d = .88$. According to Hattie, students who were offered opportunities to move at an accelerated pace through the curriculum (for example, being allowed to skip a year of school) "surpassed nonaccelerated peers of equivalent age and intelligence by nearly one grade-level" (Hattie, 2009, p. 100). While most of the research on accelerated learning conducted to date has been with gifted students, Hattie noted that some evidence suggests that *all* students may benefit from the opportunity to move through the curriculum at an accelerated pace.

That's exactly what one Chugach student whom I met several years ago did. He sprinted ahead in his high school mathematics coursework, completing it all by his sophomore year. His motivation to finish his math classes was driven, in part, by the fact that he not only enjoyed it but also wanted to carve out some extra time in his high school career to pursue his real passion: aviation. He explained that in his wild and remote part of the world, a pilot's license is almost as necessary as a driver's license is in the continental states.

In addition to letting students pace themselves through the curriculum, Chugach also employs a less-is-more approach, providing students with cross-disciplinary, hands-on activities (such as working in a simulated city, where they play roles such as architect, mayor, and judge) that help them develop deep knowledge and understanding of what they're learning. This less-is-more approach to curriculum (which is reflected in Big Picture Learning schools, career academies, and other personalized approaches profiled here) serves as an antidote to what William Schmidt and his colleagues found to be wrong with the mile-wide, inch-deep curriculum that appears to prevail in many U.S. schools. Rather than breaking the curriculum into discrete chunks of information that need to be constantly reviewed in order to be remembered, the project-based approach calls upon students to *use* their skills and knowledge to solve important problems, such as designing buildings or promoting their own communities through literature that is persuasive, visually appealing, and grammatically correct.

Five years into its transformation, Chugach could boast that its students' achievement on the state's standardized reading assessment had risen from the 28th to the 72nd percentile. Over a four-year period, schools that adopted the Chugach model through the Reinventing Schools Coalition saw their writing and mathematics scores rise an average of 27.34 and 20.94 percentage points, respectively (Delorenzo, Battino, Schreiber, & Gaddy Carrio, 2009).

Final Thoughts: A Balancing Act

Over the years, education has had its fair share of false dichotomies. Whole language versus phonics, direct instruction versus constructivism, math fundamentals versus application, site-based management versus top-down district directives—the list goes on and on. A simplistic interpretation of the Escalante and Littky stories might be that one illustrates the importance of college preparation and the other the importance of career preparation. I certainly don't want to add one more "sucker's choice" to this list, especially as neither "career preparation for all" nor "college preparation for all" is the right message to draw from these narratives.

The Importance of Challenging Curricula

At its heart, Jaime Escalante's story reflects the power of providing students with challenging curricula. Escalante believed his students were capable of learning more. When confronted with the challenge, his students rose to the occasion. That same story line has, no doubt, played out in schools across the country with equally determined teachers and students challenging themselves to learn more and go further than they (or others) thought possible. As Jay Mathews has noted, "Low-scoring schools could prepare many more students for college if they committed themselves to the task. Many high schools with large numbers of students from low-income families have done so" (Mathews, 2008b). The message of the Escalante story is that every child deserves to be given the opportunity to achieve more than he or she thought possible.

Unfortunately, challenging all students has sometimes been translated into a rigid, one-size-fits-all curriculum for all high school students. And as the dismal passing rates on the AP exam in schools that have rushed to place all students in AP classes suggest, simply challenging students does not guarantee their success. Many students require cognitive, emotional, and academic supports (the subject of the next chapter) to meet these challenges. Moreover, without adequate advisement and encouragement, students may struggle to connect long hours of AP homework with what they want to do with their lives.

The Importance of Personalizing Learning

The Littky story offers a counterbalance to translating the need to challenge students by turning higher standards into a rigid, one-size-fits-all approach to high school coursework. Littky and others like him have shown that kids succeed when they encounter personalized learning opportunities that both challenge and motivate them. In short, the answer is not a single approach or even a dichotomous choice (e.g., college preparation versus vocational education), but rather a multiple-pathways approach.

Likewise, the Escalante narrative, which demonstrates the importance of a passionate, knowledgeable instructor guiding student learning, can serve as a counterbalance to misconstruing a personalized approach to education as a wholly student-guided exploration of the world, with teachers playing a passive role as "hands-off" facilitators of student learning. As noted in the previous chapter, researchers have found little evidence supporting minimally guided instruction; lower-aptitude students, in particular, tend to benefit from more teacher-directed instruction, in which they are shown, for example, the steps required to complete an algebra problem (Kirschner, Sweller, & Clark, 2006). Yet, because direct teaching methods typically require students to put forth more effort, students tend to enjoy student-directed learning more, even while learning less from it. Left to their own devices, many students will choose the academic path of least resistance, even when it's detrimental to their own learning. As a result, personalized learning experiences can harm students, especially lower-performing ones, if they are not balanced by challenging expectations and guidance for learners, which is only gradually removed as students become more expert and self-directed learners.

Integrating Two Key Principles

To return to the discussion at the beginning of this chapter, it would appear that Aristotle and Socrates were *both* right. The lessons to be learned from high-performing elementary schools suggest that, as Aristotle held, it's important to identify and teach the body of the knowledge we want students to know so that they may acquire important foundations for future learning as well as develop self-discipline and productive habits of mind.

Yet we also know from decades of cognitive science that students (and people in general) are more apt to *master* difficult content when they are intrinsically motivated to do so. We cannot force students, of course, to be intrinsically motivated learners. Indeed, the more carrots and sticks, punishments and rewards, we foist upon them, the *less* motivated they are likely to become. The keys to intrinsic motivation are choice, autonomy, empowerment, and purpose. Students are likely to be more motivated as learners when they're given some latitude to explore, develop their own interests, and ultimately pursue what's meaningful to them—much as Socrates encouraged his band of students to look within themselves and become self-directed, lifelong seekers of knowledge.

Summarizing the Touchstones

When it comes to curriculum design—the process of determining what students should learn while they are in school—the two principles outlined above emerge from the research. These are the touchstones to which educators should consistently return when making curricular decisions:

Providing all students with high-expectations curricula. As Jaime Escalante showed in his classroom, when we set high expectations for learning, students rise to meet them. All of the effective schools and approaches described in this chapter relied heavily on standards and clearly defined (and consistently implemented) curricula that reflect high expectations for student learning.

Providing all students with personalized learning opportunities. While standards and high expectations are important, a one-size-fits-all approach to curriculum—especially one that fails to help students connect what they're learning to their own life aspirations—can undermine their intrinsic motivation for mastery learning. Littky's Big Picture Learning schools and the other successful schools and programs highlighted in this chapter have raised achievement levels and reduced dropout rates by providing students with personalized learning experiences that recognize students' need for choice, autonomy, empowerment, and purpose.

Using Standards to *Personalize* Learning

Standardization and individualization are sometimes seen as mutually exclusive. However, in practice, standards—from standard clothing sizes to standardized electrical outlets to standard formats for digital music reproduction—have led to all manner of creativity and innovation in all sorts of fields.

Consider, for example, the innumerable, personalized ways that students might demonstrate their proficiency on the following learning objective from the new Common Core standards: that students should be able to "determine central ideas or themes of a text and analyze their development; summarize the key supporting details and ideas" (National Governors Association & Council of Chief State School Officers, 2010, p. 7). Students could demonstrate their mastery of this standard in a variety of ways that could suit their personal interests: by reading and analyzing Shakespeare, Adam Smith, business plans, or contemporary political speeches, to name just a few disparate texts. The possibilities, really, are limitless. Simply stated, standards should not be the *ends* of education but, rather, just the beginning—the platform for creativity, innovation, and personalization.

One way to think about how we might integrate the two principles could be to perceive of curriculum pathways for students as something like a tree. The early grades (i.e., K–8) might be viewed as the trunk—a large, single pathway that ensures that all children receive a well-defined body of knowledge that provides them with the foundation they need to pursue any future pathway of their choosing. The success of the *It's Being Done* schools suggests that in the early grades, curriculum must be clearly articulated and reasonably uniform so that no child misses out on important learning simply because, for example, his 4th grade teacher has decided it's not important or just didn't get around to teaching it.

Certainly, choice and autonomy are helpful motivators for young students—but as noted earlier, the choices can be fairly simple, even instructionally *irrelevant,* and still have a motivational benefit. As students get older, their thinking becomes less concrete and they begin asking questions—Why do I need to know this? How is this important to me? If schools, teachers, or parents cannot provide a satisfactory answer to such questions, students are likely to become disengaged; their boredom can lead to their skipping class, and their skipping class can lead to their eventually dropping out of school altogether.

Thus, adolescence (middle or high school) is probably a good time for curricular pathways to begin branching out in different directions—simply at first, perhaps, by offering some limited, structured choices for learning (through project-based learning and the like) within a well-defined curriculum. As students continue to progress and their interests evolve, the pathways can begin to branch out more formally, giving students further opportunities to pursue their own interests.

Creating Multiple Curricular Pathways that Challenge Students: A Checklist for Curriculum Design

Setting High Expectations for Students

☐ Curriculum is "backmapped" from college/career readiness to kindergarten

☐ Curriculum identifies focused, essential content that can be reasonably taught in time available.

☐ Curriculum scope-and-sequence is identified for all core subjects and grade levels

☐ Curriculum is aligned with formative and summative assessments

☐ Model lesson plans are created for teachers to illustrate how to teach the curriculum

Personalizing Learning for Students

☐ Opportunities for structured, student-directed learning (e.g., project-based learning, structured student choices) are present in early and middle grades

☐ Career-themed curricula/pathways are offered to older (i.e., high school) students

☐ Opportunities for accelerated learning are offered to all students

☐ High-quality advisement on career and curricular pathways is offered to all students

A Word of Encouragement

For some, the idea of integrating college and career preparation and letting students choose their own pathways may seem impractical (and perhaps even a little dangerous). But as thousands of schools are now showing, such an approach is not only possible; it's getting results and changing the odds for many students nationwide.

3

Providing Whole-Child Student Supports

By most accounts, the Hurt Village housing project in Memphis, Tennessee, was a place unfit for human habitation from the late 1980s until its eventual demolition in 2002. The complex of 450 units built in the 1950s had once been celebrated as a crown jewel of urban development. (Indeed, the King himself, Elvis Presley, lived in the adjacent Lauderdale Courts complex as a teenager.)

Over the years, though, the complex became home to increasingly high concentrations of poverty, drugs, and crime. In the 1980s, the city of Memphis, lacking the funds to tear down the place, simply stopped maintaining the units, hoping that without working air-conditioners, refrigerators, or stoves the 1,000 or so inhabitants of Hurt Village would abandon it. Some did, but those who remained represented a destitute lot of poorly educated and unemployable residents, gang members, and drug addicts. On average, residents of the complex had only a 4th or 5th grade education. Only a handful held jobs; most lived on public assistance. By some estimates, as many as three-quarters suffered from mental illnesses or drug addictions. Researchers studying the Village were unable to locate a single family with two parents living under the same roof.

One child who grew up in the Village during its crime- and drug-infested nadir recalled sitting with his friends on a hillside, watching rival gangs shoot it out down below. "It was like being in the Wild West," he remembered

(Lewis, 2006, p. 271). The child, known as "Big Mike," lived with 12 other siblings from various fathers (none of whom supported the children) and a mother who had developed an addiction to crack cocaine. With her public assistance checks spent on drugs, Big Mike and his siblings were forced to forage for food from churches, school, and the street. From an early age, he spent most of his days milling about the Village, playing basketball, and seldom attending a school, a fact that in hindsight seemed inexcusable: hundreds of adults would see him wandering around, yet "no one ever said, 'What are you doing out of school?' No one ever did anything," he would later recall (p. 271).

The nights were particularly unbearable. Big Mike and his siblings slept outdoors in the summer, fending off relentless attacks from mosquitoes. Colder weather brought relief from the mosquitoes but also posed a new problem: finding a warm place to sleep. At one point, his entire family slept in an old Monte Carlo, bodies stacked like firewood on the seats and floors.

With little formal schooling, no one to read books to him at night, and his overwhelmed teachers passing him from one grade to the next regardless of whether he'd actually learned anything, Mike's IQ would eventually be tested at 80—the ninth percentile for people in general. His "ability to learn" was measured at just the sixth percentile. By the time he reached high school, he knew next to nothing. He could barely read. He didn't know the difference between a noun and verb. He didn't know basic science concepts, such as what a cell is. Nor did he know "what an ocean was, or a bird's nest, or the tooth fairy" (p. 50). He reminded his teachers of a boy who had been locked away in a closet, deprived of contact with the outside world and mainstream society.

From birth, the odds stacked against Big Mike were staggering. His environment had handed him 9 of the 13 major risk factors identified by Hodgkinson as associated with lower student achievement (see Figure 3.1):

1. He lived in poverty.

2. He was transient.

3. His mother was unemployed.

4. His mother was a single parent.

5. His mother was addicted to drugs.

6. His mother had a low level of education.

7. He lacked access to health and medical care.

8. He suffered from poor nutrition throughout most of his childhood.

9. He never experienced quality day care.

Figure 3.1
Risk Factors Associated with Lower Student Achievement

- Poverty
- Low birth weight
- Single parents
- Teen mothers
- Mothers who use alcohol, tobacco, or drugs
- Transience
- Child abuse and neglect
- Lack of high-quality day care
- Low-wage jobs for parents
- Unemployed parents
- Lack of access to health and medical care
- Low parent education levels
- Poor nutrition
- Lack of contact with English as the primary language

Source: Reprinted by permission of the Institute for Educational Leadership from Hodgkinson, H. L., *Leaving Too Many Children Behind: A Demographer's View on the Neglect of America's Youngest Children.* © 2003. All rights reserved.

Sadly, Big Mike's plight is not all that unusual. Nationwide, more than 50 percent of children are exposed to at least one "hardship" or risk factor, and 18 percent of Hispanic children and 29 percent of black children are exposed to four or more hardships. Exposure to multiple risk factors has a strong negative link to student success and accounts for nearly half of the documented achievement gap between minority and nonminority students (Duncan & Magnuson, 2005).

Low-income children exposed to multiple risk factors typically enter school already well behind their wealthier peers, scoring as much as 60 percent lower in cognitive performance than middle-income children their age; often, they arrive at kindergarten having heard or seen 30 million fewer words than most middle-income children (Neuman, 2009; see Figure 3.2).

Figure 3.2
Beginning Kindergartners' School-Readiness Skills by Socioeconomic Status (SES)

School-readiness skill	Lowest SES	Highest SES
Recognizes letters of alphabet	39%	85%
Identifies beginning sounds of words	10%	51%
Counts to twenty	48%	68%
Identifies primary colors	69%	90%
Writes own name	54%	76%
Amount of time read to prior to kindergarten	25 hours	1,000 hours
Accumulated experience with words	13 million	45 million

Source: Adapted from "From Rhetoric to Reality: The Case for High-Quality Prekindergarten Programs," by S. B. Neuman, 2003, *Phi Delta Kappan, 85*(4), 286–291.

At the age of 16, Big Mike's life took a decidedly different turn. He enrolled in a wealthy private school in the eastern suburbs of Memphis—the Briarcrest Christian Academy. The school itself, however, is not what led to the dramatic turnaround in his life. Within weeks of enrolling, many of his teachers wanted him out. He didn't just fail his tests; he wasn't even starting them. He was even failing his weight-training course—an easy grade for most students—because he wasn't bothering to suit up. For Mike, everything about his new environment—especially its high expectations for learning—was so new that he acted like an immigrant who knew neither the language nor the customs of the surroundings in which he found himself.

A new academic environment alone—even one with caring, highly effective teachers and a rigorous curriculum that challenges and engages students—is not enough to change the life trajectories of students. As Richard Rothstein, a former education columnist with the *New York Times* and now a researcher with the Economic Policy Institute, notes, "Good teachers alone, for most children, cannot fully compensate for the disadvantages many children bring to school" (Rothstein, 2010, p. 2). That's because—as James Comer, a professor at Yale University who developed the School Development Program, also known as the Comer process, has noted—a student is more than a "brain on a stick" (Comer, Haynes, & Joyner, 1996, p. 15). A variety of other factors—social, emotional, psychological, and physical—all affect his or her success as a student. Comer notes that what many students experience inside school walls is so wildly different from what they encounter outside those walls that they often struggle to adapt to the environment of school:

> A child from a poor, marginal family is likely to enter school without adequate preparation. The child may arrive without ever having learned such social skills as negotiation and compromise. A child who is expected to read at school may come from a home where no one reads and where no parent ever read a bedtime story. It is because such circumstances are at variance with mainstream expectations that these children are often considered aggressive or "bad" and often judged to be of low academic potential. (p. 16)

As some readers may have already discerned, Big Mike is Michael Oher, the principal subject of Michael Lewis's 2006 book, *The Blind Side: Evolution of a Game*, which was adapted as the 2009 film *The Blind Side*. Oher, who went on to play offensive tackle for the Baltimore Ravens, was obviously fortunate to have such phenomenal athletic talents to attract the attention of officials at the Briargate Christian Academy.

Yet, contrary to the perception that one might get from a cursory account of Oher's story (or perhaps from simply watching the movie), his story is not just that of a kid whose athletic talents made others gloss over his academic deficiencies and allowed him to skate through his studies. Indeed, both his graduation from high school and his athletic scholarship to the University of Mississippi required a phenomenal turnabout in his academic growth.

It's also worth noting that Oher's story is not that of a poor, inner-city black youth being "rescued" by a white savior, the spunky (and wealthy) Leigh Ann Tuohy (played by Sandra Bullock in the film). Oher's rescue really began when "Big Tony" Henderson, a black male who coached youth sports in inner-city Memphis, took an interest in Michael's development; it was Big Tony who first drove Michael to Briarcrest and talked officials there into enrolling him.

Simply stated, it wasn't one person who provided Michael with the supports he needed to succeed: it was a large cast of characters, who provided Michael with a heretofore absent network of support.

Indeed, the real heart of Oher's story is what can happen when a child's entire environment is dramatically altered—when the numerous factors that place him at risk for failure are replaced with a network of supports and security. The Tuohys, who eventually adopted Oher, took him off the street and gave him the first real bed he'd ever slept in (or at least didn't have to share with siblings). They also hired a tutor, Sue Mitchell, to work with him one-on-one 20 hours per week to help him catch up on all the learning he'd missed. And perhaps most important, they provided him with the emotional security of a loving family. All in all, it was a phenomenal system of supports—one that may be common among more affluent and stable families, yet often lacking for our most unfortunate kids. While reflecting on his own before-and-after story, Oher told Lewis, "I'm exactly the same guy I was back in Hurt Village. The only thing that's changed for me is the environment" (Lewis, 2006, p. 290).

Oher beat the odds. Millions of other children are not so fortunate. They come to school far less ready to learn than other children. Nor do they have the phenomenal physical gifts of a Michael Oher to help them attract the attention of wealthy benefactors who take a vested interest in their growth as human beings. For these students, high-quality instruction and challenging curricular pathways, while necessary, are not sufficient to ensure academic success.

Unfortunately, we cannot provide all disadvantaged children with a wealthy family to adopt them and provide them with the full array of financial, emotional, and academic supports that Michael Oher received. We can, however, use research to determine which social, emotional, and academic supports are most vital in mitigating the factors that place disadvantaged students at risk of failure.

An Ounce of Prevention

The first guiding principle for whole-child student supports reflects the old Benjamin Franklin adage, "An ounce of prevention is worth a pound of cure." In many ways, students' academic struggles are like a progressive disease:

harder to diagnose but easier to cure in earlier stages and easier to detect but *harder* to cure in later stages. We know from research, for example, that if students' reading struggles are left unchecked for too long, they may never catch up or they may catch up only after receiving incredibly intensive (and costly) interventions—something like the 20 hours per week of one-on-one tutoring that Michael Oher received to help him through high school.

Joseph Torgesen, a researcher at the Florida Center for Reading Research at Florida State University, has found that reading interventions aimed at 9- to 12-year-olds demonstrate mixed results at best. With enough support, these students may be able to acquire basic reading skills (such as decoding phonemes and comprehending individual words), but their fluency, or ability to read easily, may never improve—even after pulling out all the stops and providing them with up to 100 hours of one-on-one tutoring. Torgesen found that intensive interventions were helpful only for "students with very mild reading problems" but did little to catch up those who had mild, moderate, or severe reading impairments. Thus, he concludes, "If children's impairments in word-reading ability have reached moderate or severe levels, our current interventions cannot typically bring their reading fluency rates to the average range." The result of letting reading difficulties linger unchecked is, in Torgesen's words, a "devastating downward spiral." Students with early reading delays read less on their own, pick up sight words at a slower rate, learn less vocabulary and academic background knowledge, and fall even further behind (Torgesen, 2004).

The bright spot in this otherwise grim picture is the "ounce of prevention" principle, by which a downward spiral can be reversed when good instruction and remediation are provided prior to a child's 3rd grade year. After examining six studies of early reading interventions, Torgesen found that all of them brought at least half of the targeted students, who had been reading far below grade level, back to grade level within a year. One of the interventions was successful with a full 92 percent of students.

Early Childhood Programs

Research suggests that sensitive periods exist in brain development during which neural circuits are vulnerable to both negative and positive environmental influence (Rice & Barone, 2000). Many critical brain processes take shape before the age of five, well before children even enter formal schooling (Hensch, 2005). Thus, early childhood interventions are critical to student success. Kevin Gorey, an epidemiologist at the University of Windsor in Ontario, Canada, found that early childhood interventions can produce a large initial bump in children's IQ—13 to 14 points on average (Gorey, 2001).

Avoiding the Washout Effect

Researchers have long worried about a perceived "washout" effect for early childhood programs. Gorey, for example, found that five years after enrolling in early childhood programs, children's IQ scores remained higher, but just by nine points on average. Similarly, the first large-scale examination of the federally funded early childhood program Head Start concluded in 1985 that over time, the cognitive and socioemotional gains were not any greater among students enrolled in the program than among those who weren't (Olsen, 2001).

There are two points worth making here. The first is that researchers have found that although gains in IQ points do tend to fade over time, students in high-quality programs demonstrate higher levels of academic achievement well into their middle school years. Moreover, they exhibit other changes in behavior that appear to have even more lasting, positive consequences in their lives. For example, Gorey found that children who had experienced intensive early childhood interventions were less likely to be placed in special education programs as they grew up (11 percent versus 40 percent) or held back a grade (22 percent versus 43 percent) (Gorey, 2001).

The Perry Experiment

The best-known long-term study of an early childhood program is probably the Perry experiment. This study examined the long-term effects of 58 black and low-income three- and four-year-olds enrolled in an intensive early childhood program at the Perry school in Ypsilanti, Michigan, between 1962 and 1967. It tracked and compared the academic and life trajectories of these students with those of a group of 63 students not enrolled in the program.

The two-year program provided the children with two and a half hours of intensive instruction from well-trained and qualified instructors, with one teacher for every six students. In addition to working with the children, the teachers provided instruction to mothers, helping them to develop their children's language and cognitive abilities by moving beyond mere factual questions (e.g., "What color is that car?") to more open-ended, challenging questions (e.g., "What happened?" or "How did you do that?") (Rothstein, 2004).

The initial results of the experiment were discouraging. Although the average IQ of the children in the program immediately shot up by 13 points over the control group, such gains had faded by the time students reached age seven and disappeared entirely by age 10. The researchers found similar "fade-out" effects on tests of math, reading, and language.

However, at age 14, a strange thing happened: the academic scores of students in the program rebounded. A few years later, more of them went on to graduate from high school (65 percent versus 45 percent). When they entered the workplace, they had a 14 percent higher employment rate (20 percent higher for males) and were more likely to be earning over $20,000 per year (60 percent versus 40 percent). They were also half as likely to be arrested or have children out of wedlock and less likely to receive welfare or government support (Schweinhart, 2004).

Perhaps most striking, the benefits of this relatively small intervention (a 12-hour-per-week, two-year program) were still evident *40 years later,* when the students were well into midlife. Researchers calculated that after 40 years, the $15,166 initial investment per participant in the program appeared to have returned $244,812 per participant (or $16.14 for every dollar invested), measured in terms of increased income for participants and reduced public expenses for special education services, welfare, and incarceration. According to the researchers, the most lasting benefit of early childhood programs may well be their ability to help participants to develop important "non-cognitive traits"—such as persistence, commitment to schooling, self-control, and ability to delay gratification for future benefit—which supported their success later in life (Rothstein, 2004).

When examining claims about the "washout effect" of early childhood programs, it's important to consider that just like almost anything else—whether it's exercising, dieting, or learning to play the saxophone—benefits deteriorate over time if practices are not sustained. Considering that children from low-income homes are also apt to receive poor-quality instruction when they enter school, it's not surprising that the benefits of even the best early childhood programs may fade over time. It doesn't mean they're not worth doing—any more than we would say exercising daily is not worth doing just because if we stop doing it, we'll be out of shape again. High-quality early childhood programs can boost the achievement of young learners, and the gains can be sustained—the so-called washout effect avoided—if school systems continue to provide additional supports for student learning in later grades.

Real-Time Supports for Student Learning

In an analysis of the world's top-performing school systems, McKinsey & Company found that one of their distinguishing characteristics is that they consistently monitor and identify student learning and address learning difficulties as soon as they arise, providing immediate interventions to support those learning needs (McKinsey & Company, 2007). The Response to Intervention (RtI) model takes this approach, using real-time classroom-assessment data to identify students as soon as they begin to fall behind. Using a three-tier approach of increasingly intensive interventions, educators ratchet up instructional support until student learning difficulties are resolved.

Recently, *Education Week* profiled the Chula Vista Elementary School District in California for its use of RtI to produce dramatic gains in student achievement. The district, where 36 percent of students are English language learners, has been recognized by the California Association for Bilingual Education with a seal of excellence for having never missed the state's goals for adequate yearly progress—a notable feat for a district with so many students lacking fluency in English (Zehr, 2010).

By tracking student progress, identifying struggling students, and targeting real-time supports for students who most need them, the RtI approach embodies the "ounce of prevention" maxim. Instruction that is thoughtfully differentiated based on students' learning needs (as discussed in the previous chapter on challenging instruction) should be considered a frontline, default support for student learning.

Scaffolding Supports

Elena Bodrova, a McREL researcher and codeveloper of the Tools of the Mind curriculum, emphasizes the importance of scaffolding, a concept first introduced in 1976 by psychologists David Wood, Jerome Bruner, and Gail Ross (Wood, Bruner, & Ross, 1976). Bodrova writes that effective teachers provide students with scaffolding—greater support—during the early stages of learning (Bodrova, Leong, Paynter, & Hensen, 2001). Just as a building may collapse or become misshapen if the scaffolding is removed too soon, a student may develop incomplete or inaccurate knowledge or skill if the instructional supports are removed before the student is ready.

In the 1970s, Russian psychologist Lev Vygotsky identified what he called the "zone of proximal development"—a continuum of behaviors from those that students can perform independently to those they can perform with support (Vygotsky, 1978). Teachers scaffold student learning by first understanding where students are in their zone of development—identifying what they can do independently, what they can do with assistance, and what is still beyond them. Then teachers provide appropriate levels of instructional supports, or scaffolds, to help students develop their skills. As

---

Try This: Scaffolding Learning in the Classroom

The following websites provide additional information and practical guidance for scaffolding learning for young learners.

City College of New York Scaffolding Website (http://condor.admin.ccny.cuny.edu/~group4/)

This website, created by a team of professors at the City College of New York, offers articles, lesson plans, and video examples to help teachers scaffold learning in their classrooms.

McREL Scaffolding Early Literacy Website (www.mcrel.org/scaffolding-early-literacy)

Originally designed for McREL-supported grantees of the federal Early Reading First initiative, this site describes the research base behind scaffolding, provides links to research and articles on scaffolding, and offers video examples and sample lesson plans.

students demonstrate an independent ability to perform tasks and demonstrate learning, teachers gradually remove the supports. For example, for a student who is not yet capable of writing his name, the teacher may put dots on a paper in the shape of his name for the student to trace. After tracing the letters in his name, the student will begin to learn how to write them and eventually be able to write his own name without any assistance from the teacher.

Key Variables of Student Success

Although responding to student learning needs is important, simply addressing problems as they arise may feel like a futile effort for educators. Focusing only on a student's immediate needs without addressing the deeper reasons for the academic struggles is a little like a doctor prescribing cough syrup to a patient with strep: The syrup may provide some immediate relief for the sore throat, but it won't have any effect on the streptococcus bacteria that caused it.

Research points to the tremendous influence of a handful of student-level variables as the root cause of students' successes or struggles in school. Robert Marzano analyzed multiple influences on student achievement and found that fully 80 percent of the variation in student achievement can be attributed to four student-level variables (Marzano, 2000):

1. Home environment

2. Prior knowledge

3. Interest and motivation

4. Aptitude

That leaves just 20 percent of the variance in student success related to teachers (13 percent) and schools (7 percent). This information may seem disheartening to educators, who may wonder if they really can have much impact on student achievement when so much of the variance in learning comes from outside-of-school factors. However, educators should not throw up their hands in defeat. These student-level variables are *not* completely outside of their sphere of influence; indeed, to change the odds for students, school systems *must* address them. To understand how to do this, let's explore each of these influences in greater detail.

Home Environment

A recent "manifesto" signed by several superintendents of urban schools states that "the single most important factor determining whether students succeed in school is not the color of their skin or their ZIP code or even their parents' income—it is the quality of their teacher" (Klein et al., 2010). While this assertion makes for a nice sound bite, it's not entirely accurate. Teachers are the most important factor *inside* schools, but the most important factor, in general, remains the student's home environment. The good news here is that a student's home environment is not simply a function of her parents' level of income, education, or occupational status. As Marzano notes, the more malleable aspects of home environment—namely, parents' reading to their children, helping them with homework, encouraging them to go to college, and taking them to the library and cultural events—account for as much as 33 percent of the perceived variance in student achievement, far more than less malleable measures such as parents' level of income, education, and occupation (which, combined, account for only about 10 percent of the variance in student achievement) (White, 1982, cited in Marzano, 2000).

Communicating Academic Aspirations

A meta-analysis of 31 studies conducted by Fan and Chen found the single strongest factor in a student's home environment is the extent to which parents communicate high academic aspirations for their child. Indeed, the effect size of parents' communicating high expectations ($d = .87$) dwarfed the effect size ($d = .18$) of parental supervision of children (e.g., setting rules for TV watching, monitoring homework)—although the weaker perceived effects of supervision may be due, in part, to parents' setting stricter rules and bird-dogging homework only *after* children begin to struggle at school (Fan & Chen, 1999).

Nonetheless, it seems that communicating high academic expectations is one of the most important things a parent can do to support student success. Consider, for example, the story of Cedric Jennings, a young man in inner-city Washington, D.C., who overcame tremendous odds to enroll in Dartmouth University. As Ron Suskind recounts in *A Hope in the Unseen* (1998), Cedric's mother, Barbara, persistently reinforced her expectations for her son: namely, that he would make it through school and go to college—and not just *any* college, as she made plain one afternoon when Cedric was in middle school and she bought him a new sweatshirt (which she could ill afford) with "Harvard" emblazoned on the front.

Home Literacy Environment

A second variable is what researchers call the "literacy environment" of the home, which accounts for 12 to 18 percent of the variation in children's language ability (Whitehurst, 1997). In a now famous study, researchers Betty Hart and Todd Risley spent two years observing and documenting the lives of 42 "ordinary" U.S. families. They found that how parents interact with their children—in particular the number of words parents speak to the children between birth and age three and the extent to which their words are positive or negative—had a significant impact on their children's IQs and was an even bigger predictor of student success than the parents' income, education level, or social status (Hart & Risley, 1995). Hart and Risley reported that in the homes of well-educated professionals, children hear significantly more utterances and far more "encouragements" than "discouragements" (see Figure 3.3). In contrast, in low-income homes, children hear far fewer utterances and more discouragements than encouragements. As a result, lower-income children tend to develop smaller vocabularies and lower IQ scores than do children exposed to more words and encouragements at home.

Figure 3.3
Utterances Heard by Low- and High-Socioeconomic (SES) Children

	Discouragements per Hour	Affirmatives per Hour	Total Utterances per Hour	Estimated Total Utterances at Kindergarten
Lowest SES families	11	5	616	13 million
High SES families	5	32	2,153	45 million

Source: From *Meaningful Differences in the Everyday Experience of Young American Children* (pp. 125–126, 197–198), by B. Hart and R. Risley, 1995, Baltimore, MD: Paul H. Brookes Publishing.

One ray of hope in this seemingly discouraging body of research is that family literacy training has been shown to positively affect student achievement (Hanson, 2008). A meta-analysis of 16 studies of family literacy interventions found a strong, significant effect size ($d = 1.15$) for programs that provide parents with prescribed activities to work with their children on specific pre-literacy and literacy skills (Senechal & Young, 2008). One such program that has been around for nearly 40 years and shown promising results for helping low-income, minority parents improve the learning environments they provide their children at home is AVANCE (see sidebar).

Using Out-of-School Time to Address Home Environment

As Richard Rothstein notes, "The entire growth in the [achievement] gap during the years children are in school develops during the summer months" (Rothstein, 2004, p. 57). During the regular school year, children from low-income homes appear to progress at the same rate as children from middle- and high-income homes, yet they "fall behind in summer, either because middle-class children learn more or forget less in the summer months" (p. 57). For example, Rothstein cites one study of New York City children conducted 40 years ago that found that while white children learned at a rate about one-fourth as fast during the summer as during the regular school year, black children learned only one-sixteenth as fast; although these data are dated, Rothstein notes that "other studies have since confirmed these results" (p. 57).

The implications of this research seem clear. If we could provide disadvantaged children with learning experiences similar to what more advantaged children typically receive during the summer—when they enroll in camps, take trips to libraries and museums, and develop

---

A Closer Look: AVANCE

AVANCE is a nonprofit program that is designed to help immigrant families break the cycle of poverty by working with parents to improve the home learning environments they provide their children. Begun in the early 1970s in San Antonio, it has active programs in Texas, California, and New Mexico.

The program targets low-income families, many of whom experienced poor home environments themselves as children. Through a series of 27 lessons, it teaches parents to create safe, stable, and language-rich home environments for their children.

While no recent external evaluation has been conducted of the program, the organization self-reports promising results in Dallas and El Paso. In Dallas, for example, students whose families are in the program had a 99 percent attendance rate—far higher than the district average. They also demonstrated higher rates of proficiency on state assessments—88 percent proficient in reading versus 73 percent districtwide, and 82 percent proficient in math versus 60 percent proficient in the district.

More information about the program and its results is available on the AVANCE website at www .avance.org.

The National Center for Quality Afterschool Learning (http://www.sedl.org/afterschool)

Led by SEDL, in Austin, Texas, and joined by partners CRESST, McREL, Learning Point Associates, Education Northwest, SERVE, and WGBH, the federally funded National Partnership for Quality Afterschool Learning studied afterschool programs nationwide and identified exemplary practices of the most effective programs. Based on this research, the partners developed practical guidance for educators, which is now available free online—including a database of lesson plans and videos of effective afterschool programs.

IES Practice Guide: Structuring Out-of-School-Time to Improve Academic Achievement (http://ies.ed.gov/ncee/wwc/pdf/practiceguides/ost_pg_072109.pdf)

This free guide from the U.S. Department of Education's Institute of Education Sciences provides five practical recommendations to help school and district leaders, out-of-school program coordinators, and teachers design out-of-school-time programs that boost student achievement.

their talents in music, art, and sports—we could likely boost the summer learning rates of less-advantaged students to be more on par with that of their more advantaged peers. In so doing, we could reduce their summer learning gaps.

Health Issues

A number of health issues related to home environment place low-income students at risk. Asthma, for example, afflicts low-income students at disproportionate rates; left untreated, it can lead to hospitalization and absences from school. Researchers have found that schoolchildren with asthma who attend a school with a school-based clinic miss fewer days of school than those who attend school without such a center (Webber et al., 2003).

Poor eyesight is another concern. Left untreated it, too, can diminish student achievement. A six-year demonstration study conducted several years ago in the Boston area found that the simple intervention of correcting the eyesight of low-income students increased their achievement by 4.5 percentile points (Rothstein, 2004).

Finally, a nationwide survey of students found that a variety of factors—including adolescence, being male, receiving public assistance for health care (likely a proxy for income), being from a one-parent family, and parental depression—all place youth at higher risk for depression. And though disadvantaged youth are more susceptible to mental health problems, researchers have found that they are *less likely* to visit mental health professionals than are their peers. Of course, if left unchecked, depression increases the likelihood that a student will drop out of school, abuse drugs or alcohol, and commit suicide (Howell & McFeeters, 2008).

School-based health clinics that address these issues have been shown to reduce absenteeism, tardiness, truancy, and dropout rates for students (Flaherty & Weist, 1999). Indeed, studies have found that youth are 10 to 21 times more likely to access mental health services if they are provided at a school-based clinic (Juszczak, Melinkovich, & Kaplan, 2003).

One large-scale example of an organization taking a multifaceted approach to addressing children's home environments is the Harlem Children's Zone (HCZ). Approximately 10,000 children live in the one square mile that is called the Zone; nearly all live in poverty, and two-thirds score below grade level on standardized tests. The Zone's director, Geoffrey Canada, has poured social, medical, and educational services into the area and has guaranteed parents that their children will get into college if they hold up their end of the bargain and get their children to school. Canada's model, the HCZ Pipeline, provides uninterrupted support for the healthy development of children in the Zone—from conception to graduation from college. Anchored by a "Baby College" for expecting parents, and including a prekindergarten component, the HCZ Pipeline is different from other initiatives in its unwavering determination to reengineer the physical, social, and home environments in which children reside (Tough, 2009).

Prior Knowledge

Robert Marzano (2000) found that students' background knowledge, or "prior knowledge," accounts for approximately 41 percent of the variance in student achievement—an effect size of $d = 1.81$. Much like the strong influence of home environment, this statistic may also discourage educators at first blush. What, after all,

---

A Closer Look: School-Based Health Clinics

In a 2009 article in *American Educator* magazine, Jane Quinn of the Children's Aid Society and author Joy Dryfoos profiled the following schools and districts where school-based health clinics appear to be having positive effects for students, including in supporting higher levels of student achievement:

- Chicago Community Schools Initiative
- Gardner Pilot Academy, Boston, Massachusetts
- Kendall-Whittier Elementary School, Tulsa, Oklahoma
- P.S. 5, P.S. 8, P.S./I.S. 50, and Salome Ureña de Henriquez Campus, New York City, New York
- Schools Uniting Neighborhoods, Multnomah, Oregon

Online Resources

Model programs for school-based health clinics, technical assistance, and information about funding and resourcing clinics are available on the National Assembly on School Based Health Care website at www.nasbhc.org.

Source: From "Freeing Teachers to Teach: Students in Full-Service Community Schools Are Ready to Learn," by J. Quinn and J. Dryfoos, 2009, *American Educator, 33*(2), 16–21.

A Closer Look: Emery Unified School District: A Cash-Strapped District Offers Whole-Child Supports

For districts that are scrambling to fill budget gaps, offering a comprehensive array of services for students may be far down the list of priorities—somewhere after figuring out how to cover teacher salaries, absorb rising pension costs, and mollify angry parents when schools are closed.

Emery Unified School District in California, however, provides an example of a district that actually used a financial crisis—it declared bankruptcy in 2001—to enlist support from the community and develop a system of whole-child student supports.

Granted, the district is small (just two schools and 780 students) and benefits from having some well-heeled companies within its borders. Yet the needs are great: 84 percent of its students qualify for free or reduced-price lunches. To help address deficits in students' home environments, then superintendent Tony Smith (who took the helm of Oakland Unified School District in 2009) reached out to local businesses and organizations, such as Pixar, Novartis, the Y.M.C.A., and the University of California–Berkeley, to develop a network of supports for students.

"Children in affluent families are provided a certain environment that plays a powerful role," Mr.

Continued on next page >

can schools or teachers do about the level of knowledge students bring to the classroom?

Plenty, as it turns out. A growing body of research points to systematic vocabulary instruction as an effective way to narrow the gap for students who are economically disadvantaged, second-language learners, and those who have learning disabilities (Storch & Whitehurst, 2002). As 19th-century clergyman Henry Ward Beecher noted long ago, "All words are pegs to hang ideas on." Expanding students' vocabularies in terms of content (ensuring, for example, that they understand the meaning of such words as *photosynthesis* and *denominator*) and academics (ensuring they know the difference between *summarize* and *synthesize*) provides the "pegs" upon which students can hang ideas and expand their knowledge.

Stone and Urquhart (2008) report that better readers may learn as many as seven new words a day, while struggling readers may pick up only one or two new words (see sidebar). Students with stronger vocabularies are more prone to enjoy reading, thus reading more and expanding their vocabularies. Conversely, students who encounter many words they do not know in a text are less prone to enjoy reading and thus, read less. As a result, a yawning gap in reading proficiency and vocabulary development begins to appear between proficient and struggling readers. One way to close this gap is through intentional vocabulary instruction—that is, directly teaching new terms that are critical to learning content—which research has shown can have a significant, positive impact on student achievement. Of course, not all words are equally important or demand the same amount of instruction time. One approach to focusing vocabulary instruction is to identify key terms embedded in standards and benchmarks and to ensure that students understand these terms.

Interest and Motivation

It stands to reason that students who are more motivated to learn do better in school than those who are less motivated. As Marzano (2000) notes, "student interest" has a moderate to strong influence on student success, accounting for approximately 14 percent of the observed variance in achievement.

Fate Control

In his book *So Much Reform, So Little Change: The Persistence of Failure in Urban Schools*, University of Chicago professor (and newly appointed chief academic officer of Chicago Public Schools) Charles Payne writes that an often-overlooked success factor for many students is what James Coleman identified in the famous (or to some, infamous) Coleman report of 1966: "fate control"—that is, students' belief in their ability to guide and shape their own destinies (Payne, 2008). Coleman determined that fate control had a stronger relationship to student achievement than all school-related factors combined. Other researchers have since found that minorities (with the exception of Asian students) tend to have a much weaker sense of fate control than white students. As Payne writes, "It seems that black students are more prone to see themselves as objects rather than subjects"—that is, they are more likely to believe that how hard they try in their studies is of little consequence, and thus they put forth less effort in school (p. 110).

Stereotype Threat

Payne also writes about the deleterious effect that "stereotype threat" can have on minority student achievement. Surveys of suburban black students have found that they are often intensely worried about whether other students and teachers will perceive them as less

---

A Closer Look: Emery Unified School District: A Cash-Strapped District Offers Whole-Child Supports (continued)

Smith told the *New York Times*. "Those opportunities don't always exist for our children."

Smith, inspired by the Harlem Children's Zone, has begun to reach out to businesses and neighborhood organizations to create a similar network of student supports in Oakland. He acknowledges that the work isn't easy, yet it's vitally important. "It's a big, crazy, intense idea that we would do this citywide," Smith told the *Times*. "Yet the pattern we see now is unacceptable, and unless we do something significantly different, we're not going to get a different outcome."

Source: From "Emeryville May Point the Way Up," by G. Shih, July 22, 2010, *New York Times*. Retrieved from http://www.nytimes.com/2010/07/23/us/23bcemeryville.html?_r=2&pagewanted=print

Try This: A Five-Step Process for Direct Vocabulary Instruction

After identifying critical vocabulary terms students need to know in order to understand important concepts they will encounter, teachers can use this five-step process to teach these words to students.

Step 1: Present students with a brief explanation or description of the new term or phrase. State the meaning of the word in student-friendly language to help learners develop a basic understanding of the word.

Step 2: Present students with a non-linguistic representation of the new term or phrase. The more students can visualize terms, the better they are able to recall them later.

Step 3: Ask students to generate their own explanation or description of the term or phrase. Initiate student thinking about words by using sentence stems such as these:

• It is kind of like …

• It looks like …

• It is when you …

Step 4: Ask students to create their own nonlinguistic representation of the term or phrase.

Students might use graphic organizers, mental maps and models, physical representations, or kinesthetic representations to depict terms.

Step 5: Periodically ask students to review the accuracy of their explanations and representations. Help

Continued on next page ❯

smart than their white peers. They become afraid to ask questions in class or seek extra help from teachers out of fear that doing so will somehow demonstrate their lack of intelligence or reinforce a negative stereotype. This sort of anxiety is not altogether dissimilar from the fixed view of intelligence that Stanford psychologist Carol Dweck found could lead students to exert less effort out of fear of revealing their lack of intelligence (Dweck, 2006).

Student motivation can be a thorny topic—one that some are reluctant to bring up, lest it lead to blaming the victims. However, when we understand that stereotype threat and fate control may be underlying reasons why some students don't apply themselves at school, we can begin to find ways to overcome these barriers and unlock their motivation.

One simple way that classroom teachers can help to counteract a lack of fate control and encourage motivation is to help students set short-term learning goals (e.g., increasing the number of math problems they can do in a minute) and help them track their progress toward their goals, all the while highlighting the important link between effort and results.

Using Out-of-School Time to Create a Sense of Self-Efficacy and Fate Control

Here again, it seems that well-designed afterschool and summer programs may help to address another critical student-level variable. By providing students with opportunities to develop mastery experiences in areas such as music, art, or physical fitness, students can begin to see how effort and practice lead to tangible results— for example, learning how to play a guitar, perform a choreographed dance, or clear a high-jump bar. Indeed, Richard Rothstein asserts that a key focus of summer and afterschool programs should be to replicate the kinds of experiences that more advantaged children enjoy outside of school:

> An education that hopes to narrow the achievement gap significantly, therefore, should provide comparable summer experiences—not only a summer school of extra drill in reading and math and not even a summer school only of more advanced academic skills. Art, music, drama, dance, and physical education teachers should be more numerous in the summer than in the regular year. (Rothstein, 2004, pp. 143–144)

Some educators might question why out-of-school-time programs should focus on nonacademic learning at all. After all, if kids are falling behind in school, shouldn't they be spending their extra hours in a sort of academic "boot camp" that whips them back into shape?

Certainly, some academic learning can be part of out-of-school-time programs. Yet if the root cause of a child's low academic performance is a weak sense of self-efficacy or fate control, simply thrusting flash cards in her face is not likely to cause a dramatic turnabout in her learning. On the other hand, teaching her something that she's intrinsically motivated to master—for example, learning how to play a guitar—can show her that through practice, she can develop new talents. Later, she can draw upon this experience when she encounters challenges in school (e.g., "If I can learn how to play an A minor ninth jazz chord, surely I can figure out the quadratic formula"). Ultimately, she may begin to see that through hard work and effort, she can accomplish even larger goals, such as graduating from high school and going on to college.

Combating Stereotype Threat by Creating Growth Mind-Sets

Reinforcing the value of effort and downplaying the importance of intelligence—which is the essence of

---

Try This: A Five-Step Process for Direct Vocabulary Instruction (continued)

students recall vocabulary words later by modeling for them how to use a list of questions to review and refine their understanding of words they've learned. For example, they might ask themselves, "Does my prior understanding of a word still hold up? Is there anything that is incorrect or inaccurate? Do I need to change how I have represented my understanding?"

Source: Adapted from *Remove Limits to Learning with Systematic Vocabulary Instruction*, by B. J. Stone and V. Urquhart, 2008, Denver, CO: McREL.

conveying a "growth mind-set" in the classroom—may help to allay student anxieties rooted in stereotype threat. If teachers encourage all of their students to demonstrate a desire to grow smarter by asking questions and taking on new challenges (even if it means failing on a regular basis), they can give license to students to seek help—especially those who might fear that doing so could make them look "dumb."

Looking Inside the Brain: Unlocking the Mysteries of Motivation

While we've addressed two factors—lack of fate control and stereotype threat—that appear to *discourage* motivation in some students, the question still remains: What gives some people a deep inner drive to succeed? Michael Oher, for example, believed from an early age that he would be the next Michael Jordan and practiced basketball 10 to 12 hours a day (until he eventually reconciled himself to the fact that his 300-plus pounds made it unlikely he would find himself in the NBA and redirected his dream to the NFL). Certainly, educators would prefer that students set more academic goals for themselves (for example, becoming a NASA engineer or poet laureate). Nonetheless, Oher's intrinsic motivation to succeed in sports was a large part of what propelled him through his grueling regime of 20-plus hours of extra schoolwork per week—on top of attending school and practicing sports.

So why is it that some students, like Oher, have a profound motivation to succeed—no matter what obstacles or discouragements are placed in their way—while others become quickly discouraged and resigned to failure?

Until recently, it's been difficult to ascertain exactly what causes one student to develop the self-discipline and persistence necessary to work hard and succeed in school. New brain research, however, has begun to unlock the mystery of motivation. It suggests that the heretofore "hidden" source of motivation may reside in a part of the brain called the "rostral lateral prefrontal cortex." It's the part of the brain that appears to set humans apart from apes, providing us with the ability to set goals, regulate our behavior, and maintain concentration, which is something scientists and psychologists call "executive function."

Researchers have found that children's ability to demonstrate executive function is more predictive of school readiness than IQ or entry-level mathematics and reading skills (Blair & Razza, 2007). Executive function skills—namely, self-monitoring, self-control, persistence, and self-regulation—have also been singled out as key predictors of college readiness (Conley, 2007). Conversely, poor self-regulation is predictive of school problems like aggression, juvenile delinquency, and dropping out (Schunk, 2005).

Developing Self-Regulation Through Dramatic Play

Here again, there's an upside. With the right interventions, young children can develop critical executive-function skills. One of the most effective ways to develop these skills is something that children have been doing for generations: engaging in dramatic play. McREL's Scaffolding Early Learning (SEL) program, for example, is specifically designed to help children develop their ability to regulate their own social and cognitive behaviors. In SEL classrooms, teachers are equipped with a set of special strategies to increase the value of make-believe play. Teachers learn how to stage various play centers in the classroom, where children might pretend to run a bookstore, work together as firefighters to put out a fire, or serve as the crew and passengers of an airplane (Bodrova, Leong, Paynter, & Hensen, 2003). Prior to joining the play center, each child develops a "play plan" (presented as a drawing, writing, or dictation to the teacher) that identifies the role he or she will play. Throughout the play period, which lasts for up to an hour (an eternity for many four-year-olds), children must stay in their roles and learn to correct one another when someone slips out of character. As a result, they develop the ability to regulate their behavior, think creatively and abstractly (using a wooden block, for example, to represent the nozzle of a fire hose), and focus on the same task for an hour or more.

A recent study of the SEL program found that, at the end of two years, children enrolled in it outperformed a control group of children on four tests of executive function. In some locations, the program has become a victim of its own success. As Bronson and Merryman (2009) report, the Tools of the Mind curriculum (a manifestation of the SEL program) has been so effective in Elgin, Illinois, and Midland, Texas, that the grant to study it was rescinded because the children in the program no longer scored low enough for them to be considered at risk. McREL principal researcher Elena Bodrova, who is quick to credit teachers for students' success, told Bronson and Merryman, "When it keeps happening enough times, you start to think that it may be our program that makes the difference. It's the irony of doing interventions in the real world: being too successful to study if it's successful" (p. 165).

Aptitude

A final consideration of student-level factors, is, of course, aptitude—stated plainly, a child's smarts. Popular perception may hold that there's no substitute for IQ points when it comes to student success. However, when the confounding variables of school, classroom, and home environment are factored out, a correlation of about .25 exists between a student's innate intelligence as measured by IQ tests and performance on standardized achievement tests (Marzano, 2000). If we follow the simple formula for translating a correlation into percentage variance, squaring the correlation (i.e., multiplying .25 by .25), we find that only about 6.25 percent of the observed variance in student achievement is attributable to innate intelligence. This relatively weak correlation between aptitude and student success may come as a surprise to some, as it appears to contradict the conventional wisdom that it's "smart" kids who do well in school. However, as noted in Chapter 1, new research on the brain is finding that intelligence is not a fixed phenomenon; rather, it is something that grows over time. It seems that conventional wisdom has it exactly backward: It's not that smart kids do well in school, it's that kids who do well in school get smart.

Returning to the Touchstones

A pair of key principles bubble up from the research that should guide school systems' thinking about how to provide struggling students with the additional supports they need for success:

Providing real-time supports in keeping with the ounce-of-prevention principle. Learning difficulties are far simpler to address early, before students enter a downward spiral of poor performance. If left unchecked too long, learning difficulties may snowball to a point that even the most intensive (and costly) of interventions will produce, at best, mixed results.

Addressing the deep causes of student performance: home environment, prior knowledge, interest, and motivation. Educators should not consider the student-level influences of environment, background knowledge, and motivation (which account for as much as 80 percent of the variance in student achievement) as outside their sphere of influence. Indeed, numerous programs and interventions have been shown to positively address all three.

Testing the Touchstones: A $1 Billion Lesson

This chapter has identified a pair of touchstones of student supports—first, providing supports early and in real-time response to student learning needs and second, addressing the key student-level variables that account for the bulk of the variance in student achievement.

The failure of a $1 billion investment in schools to move the needle of student achievement offers us a laboratory in which to test the touchstones. In the late 1990s, the federal government launched the 21st Century Community Learning Centers program, a $40 million effort that grew into a $1 billion investment to provide students with a safe place to go after school to improve their achievement. A nationwide evaluation of the centers in 2005 found "wide variability in activities and services delivered across programs" and little "coordination with the school-day curriculum" (James-Burdumy et al., 2005, p. xxii). As a result, students randomly assigned to the afterschool centers reported that they felt safer after school but demonstrated no higher levels of achievement than students in the control group—a disappointing result, to say the least, for a $1 billion outlay.

That's not to say that afterschool or summer and weekend programs never work. In 2006, McREL conducted a meta-analysis of 56 rigorous research studies on out-of-school-time programs (Lauer et al., 2004). The study found a small but significant effect size for K–2 reading programs ($d = .25$) and a larger effect size ($d = .44$) for programs designed to improve high school

---

Whole-Child Student Supports: A Checklist for Teachers

A key point of this chapter is that teachers alone cannot address all of the factors that contribute to truly disadvantaged students' low levels of achievement—a systemic response to students' early learning and ongoing social, emotional, and physical needs is required. Nonetheless, teachers don't need to wait for someone else to help their students. This checklist identifies some simple things that teachers can do in their classrooms to provide whole-child supports for students.

Provide real-time supports in keeping with the ounce-of-prevention principle

☐ Use formative assessments (or regular checks for understanding) to identify student learning needs

☐ Use a Response to Intervention approach to provide more intensive instruction as needed

Address the deep causes of student performance

☐ Students set and realize short-term goals to develop a sense of fate control

☐ Teachers communicate growth mind-sets in the classroom to encourage student motivation and dispel stereotype-threat anxieties

☐ Teachers use direct vocabulary instruction to fill gaps in students' prior knowledge

☐ Teachers correspond regularly with parents to help them create positive home learning environments

students' mathematics achievement. As in the 21st Century Community Learning Centers evaluation study, McREL also found a wide variation in the quality of afterschool and summer school programs. In general, though, McREL found that when out-of-school-time programs work, it's because they

- Provide one-on-one tutoring in reading.

- Combine recreation with learning—for example, providing natural-science field trips, gardening, sports, and cultural activities with learning.

- Develop student motivation—for example, by providing high school students with classes held on a college campus so that they begin to see themselves as college-bound.

It appears, then, that effective out-of-school programs offer real-time supports while also directly addressing many student-level influences on achievement that educators might otherwise believe are outside their sphere of influence. Specifically, effective out-of-school-time programs

- Provide students who are falling behind with *real-time academic supports* through individual tutoring that can prevent them from falling further behind.

- Supplement students' *home environments* by offering the kind of homework support that more advantaged children are likely to receive at home.

- Build students' *prior knowledge* and *aptitude* with enrichment activities such as field trips, gardening, and cultural exposure that advantaged students are more likely to receive at home.

- Address students' *interest* and *motivation to learn* by making learning fun and providing students with the opportunity to experience college firsthand.

While the 21st Century Community Learning Centers program has been revised to more closely align with best practices, an important (albeit expensive) lesson that we could draw from it is that extended learning opportunities, including afterschool, weekend, and summer programs, should not simply provide custodial care for students or deliver "more of the same" that they receive during the day. Rather, these extra hours afford a unique opportunity to provide whole-child student supports that address the most critical variables discussed here.

Final Thoughts: A Useful Medical Metaphor

The underlying principles of student supports really boil down to two simple ideas: diagnose and address student struggles early; and, where possible, treat the root causes of any failures (e.g., lack of academic vocabulary or background knowledge), not just the surface symptoms (e.g., poor performance in the classroom).

A useful metaphor here may be that of health care. Like doctors in an emergency room providing triage, educators must respond in real time, providing supports that students need *now* to keep from falling further behind. However, unless educators act proactively rather than reactively, they will remain in a perpetual state of emergency. Indeed, just as when doctors diagnose a problem early they can prevent visits to the emergency room, school systems may also be able to head off more serious learning issues by addressing the powerful, student-level variables that students bring to school with them every day. And ultimately, by providing the right network of student supports, they can make the uncommonly inspiring stories of students like Michael Oher or Cedric Jennings a more common narrative for all children.

4

Creating High-Performance School Cultures

In *Everyday Survival: Why Smart People Do Stupid Things* (2009), Laurence Gonzalez recounts how, through trial and error, aviation pioneers arrived at a counterintuitive solution for dealing with one of the most frightening events that can occur to a pilot:

> In the early days of aviation, the spin was a mysterious event, a death spiral from which pilots rarely recovered. Knowing that, a pilot who found himself in a spin would bail out if he happened to be blessed with a parachute. And then people began to notice something strange. After the pilot bailed out, the plane would sometimes right itself and fly on until it crashed or ran out of fuel. A clever pilot proposed this: the airplane wasn't at fault. The pilot was doing something to keep the airplane in the spin. Remove the pilot, and you solve the problem. Pilots began to learn how to recover from spins by doing less, not more. (p. 44)

The problem: Pilots' frantically thrashing about at the controls exacerbated the spin stall. The solution: Engage in a few calm, controlled, and fluid movements to right the plane.

Low-performing schools can similarly benefit from doing less, not more. A few years ago, a colleague and I examined several improvement plans from around the country. Instead of focusing on a small handful of well-defined, high-impact efforts, we found that most of the plans laid out a dizzying array of initiatives, with several action items for each. Some identified as many as 30 to 40 actions for a single year. That's nearly one per week!

Like pilots in those early open-seat biplanes, it would appear that many schools in the "spin stall" of low student performance appear to be frantically thrashing about at the controls—implementing reading, writing, and math programs; bringing teachers together to sift through data and make what they hope to be data-driven decisions; creating new teacher committees to focus on specific student needs; exploring new ways to engage parents in decision making; adopting new programs to improve student behavior and motivation; and bringing in experts on all manner of topics. And when there's time, they may work on improving instruction.

Obviously, that's far too much activity for any school staff to juggle or take seriously. As a result, usually very little happens. The school continues spinning out of control, which only leads to more anxiety and thrashing about, with minimal, if any, improvement. What educators achieve instead is a state of exhaustion and a metastasizing sense of hopelessness.

More Bang for the Buck: Reducing Variability in Teaching Quality

School leaders would do well to recognize that many of the things they might be tempted to put into a school improvement plan have, at best, only limited influence on student achievement. To make this point, Figure 4.1 depicts several school-level influences from John Hattie and other sources that have been categorized according to Hattie's "hinge point" effect size of $d = .40$ (see the Introduction for more about the hinge point).

As these data show, few school-level influences stand out as critical to student achievement (the exceptions being aligning curriculum with assessments [opportunity to learn] and adopting programs to reduce disruptive behavior in classrooms). That's not surprising, though, given that school-level factors account for only about 7 percent of the variance in student achievement, while teacher influences account for 13 percent and student-level influences for fully 80 percent (Marzano, 2000).

For the most part, school-level influences tend to be distal, or indirect, influences on achievement, whereas changes in classroom environments tend

Figure 4.1
Selected School-Level Influences on Student Achievement

Strong Influence *Effect sizes above* *d = .40*		Moderate Influence *Effect sizes between* *d = .20 and .40*		Weak Influence *Effect sizes below* *d = .20*	
Influence	ES	Influence	ES	Influence	ES
Opportunity to learn (*aligning curriculum to assessments and monitoring its use in classrooms*)[1]	.88	Optimizing instruction time (*maximizing time spent teaching, minimizing distractions*)[1]	.39	Class size (*reducing classes from 25 to 15 students*)[2]	.13
Decreasing disruptive behavior (*programs to address behavior issues*)[2]	.85*	Clear and monitored achievement goals (*articulating and monitoring schoolwide achievement goals*)[1]	.30	Ability grouping (*tracking students into different classes by ability*)[2]	.12
Leadership (*schools with leaders who receive high teacher ratings on key leadership behaviors*)[3]	.52	Pressure to achieve (*communicating academic success as a primary school goal*)[1]	.27	Afterschool programs (*out-of-school-time learning experiences, on average*)[4]	.09
School size (*high school size between 600 and 900 students*)[2]	.43	Parental involvement (*involving parents in setting and enforcing policies*)[1]	.26	Cooperation (*encouraging professionalism among teachers*)[1]	.06
		School climate (*clearly articulating and enforcing rules of behavior*)[1]	.22	Multi-age classrooms (*placing students of different ages/grade levels in the same classroom*)[2]	.04
				Open classrooms (*open classroom architecture and individualized instruction*)[2]	.01

[1] Marzano, R. J. (2000). *A new era of school reform: Going where the research takes us.* Aurora, CO: Mid-continent Research for Education and Learning.
[2] Hattie, J. (2009). *Visible learning: A synthesis of over 800 meta-analyses relating to achievement.* New York: Routledge.
[3] Waters, J. T., Marzano, R. J., & McNulty, B. A. (2003). *Balanced leadership: What 30 years of research tells us about the effect of leadership on student achievement.* Aurora, CO: Mid-continent Research for Education and Learning. (*Note:* This report stated the *correlation* of leadership as *r* = .25. For comparative purposes, that correlation coefficient has been translated here as a Cohen's *d* effect size of *d* = .52.)
[4] Lauer, P. A., Akiba, M., Wilkerson, S. B., Apthorp, H. S., Snow, D., & Martin-Glenn, M. (2004). *The effectiveness of out-of-school-time strategies in assisting low-achieving students in reading and mathematics: A research synthesis* (rev. ed.). Aurora, CO: Mid-continent Research for Education and Learning.
* Restated from Hattie's *Visible Learning*, which reports an effect size of *d* = .34. Hattie's number includes results of a meta-analysis that simply measured influence of behavioral issues on student achievement—not programs designed to address those issues. Removing the results of this one meta-analysis yields a much higher effect size.

to have a more direct and immediate effect. For example, clearly articulating and enforcing rules of behavior at the school level has an effect size of $d = .22$, whereas decreasing disruptive behavior in the classroom and using effective classroom-management strategies have effect sizes of $d = .85$ and $d = .52$, respectively (Marzano, Marzano, & Pickering, 2003).

Variability in Teaching Quality

Like starlight, it would appear that school-level changes become more diffuse as they spread out to classrooms, where they are implemented well or poorly but almost certainly unevenly, given the well-documented uneven quality of classroom learning environments. As I noted earlier, researchers have found that a great deal of variance exists in the quality of learning experiences students receive—even within the same school. One examination of surveys and achievement data for more than 54,000 students over the past 30 years found "considerable teacher heterogeneity" in the sample (Konstantopoulos, 2005, p. 1). Specifically, the researchers found that variances in teaching quality accounted for much more of the variance in student achievement (in some cases, as much as twice the effect) than variances in school quality. Such a finding suggests that instead of effective (or ineffective) teachers being clustered together in the same schools, they appear to be dispersed, leaving most schools with a mix of both high- and low-quality teachers.

This is important because, as Hanushek (1998) has noted, teaching quality trumps almost everything else occurring in a school. He arrived at this conclusion after analyzing more than 100 studies of class size–reduction initiatives and finding that any benefits from reductions in class sizes were wiped out when teacher hiring sprees resulted in decreases to teacher quality. The bottom line is that variations in teacher quality "completely dominate any effects of altered class sizes" (p. 35).

Getting More Bang for the Buck

What all of this means is that schools will likely get more "bang for the buck" from improvement efforts if they focus on guaranteeing high-quality instruction across the entire school. A McREL meta-analysis of research on effective school leaders identified several leadership responsibilities explicitly

Try This: Using Classroom Walkthroughs to Reduce Variance in Teaching Quality

For some, the practice of classroom "walkthroughs," where principals spend a few minutes observing classrooms to form an impression about the quality of teaching occurring in them, may seem preposterous. But consider for a moment the study that Malcolm Gladwell describes in his book *Blink* (2005).

After watching just two seconds of soundless video clips of Harvard professors teaching a class, students were asked to rate how effective they believed the professors would be as instructors. Here's the surprising result: the students' instantaneous impressions were nearly identical to those that other students made after being in class with the professors for an entire semester. So if college students can accurately assess the quality of professors from just two seconds of video, can principals gauge the quality of teaching after a few minutes in the classroom?

Perhaps. But the key to making accurate decisions based on short observations lies in knowing what to look for. For example, when emergency room personnel in the Cook County Hospital reduced their lengthy interview protocol for chest-pain patients down to a single EKG reading and three (more incisive) questions, they *increased* their ability to accurately

Continued on next page ❯

related to improving instructional quality. In particular, strong links were found between student success and leaders who

- Are *directly* involved in the design and implementation of curriculum, instruction, and assessment practices.

- Protect teachers from issues or influences that might otherwise detract from their teaching.

- Provide teachers with the resources and materials (including staff development) they need to deliver high-quality instruction and effectively manage their classrooms (Marzano, Waters, & McNulty, 2005).

In addition, Robinson, Lloyd, and Rowe (2008) found that leadership behaviors that focus directly on teacher development activities have two to three times more effect on student achievement than behaviors focused on organizational development, including ensuring an orderly and supportive school environment, aligning resources to teaching goals, coordinating curriculum implementation, and establishing school-level goals and expectations.

It would appear, then, that "job one" of principals should be to reduce the variability in teaching quality within their schools. This means visiting classrooms, observing teaching (see sidebar), coaching teachers to higher levels of performance, evaluating their performance, and supporting their professional development.

A Caveat: Don't Neglect Organizational Development

Although the effect sizes for organizational development leadership activities are smaller than those for teacher development activities, they're not inconsequential—all of them are close to or greater than Hattie's hinge point. Moreover, they are effect sizes for leadership behaviors across the board, including high-, average-, and low-performing schools. So diminished effect size for some practices may simply mean that these behaviors are less important in particular environments. For example, in schools that already have an orderly environment, maintaining order is probably necessary to keep achievement from dipping but likely won't result in significant gains in student performance. On the other hand, focusing on turning an unsafe school into an orderly one may be exactly what the doctor ordered. The point is that focusing on teacher development appears to be good practice in nearly every school environment.

Finally, it's worth noting that even smaller effect-size influences can dramatically transform school performance; that is, the whole may be greater than the sum of the parts, if they are integrated in thoughtful and strategic ways. To illustrate the impact that smaller effect-size influences can have when they are put to bigger ends, let's turn to an example that Malcolm Gladwell provides in *The Tipping Point: How Little Things Can Make a Big Difference* (2000)—namely, the Broken Windows theory.

Broken Windows Theory and School Culture

In the mid-1980s, New York City resembled an airplane in a spin stall. Crime rates were skyrocketing, with the city averaging more than 2,000 murders and 600,000 serious crimes each year. In the words of one observer, entering the subway system was like "going into the transit version of Dante's *Inferno*" (p. 137). The subways were home to more than 15,000 felonies each year. Aggressive panhandling, pickpocketing, and petty crimes—including gang members' forcing passengers to pay *them* to enter—were commonplace.

Try This: Using Classroom Walkthroughs to Reduce Variance in Teaching Quality (continued)

diagnose if patients were about to have a heart attack. The same principle may be true for classroom observations. If principals have the right set of "look fors" and a clear understanding of the purposes of walkthroughs, brief classroom observation can, in fact, be a powerful tool for promoting great teaching.

Here are some questions that principals should ask when observing classrooms:

Are teachers using research-based teaching strategies? Principals might use Marzano, Pickering, and Pollock's *Classroom Instruction that Works* (2001) as a framework to determine the extent to which teachers are using research-based instructional strategies. However, great teachers not only use research-based instructional strategies but also understand their purposes and can articulate in follow-up conversations *why* they used a particular strategy.

Do students understand their goals for learning? Can students articulate the task as it relates to learning goals? Are they making a connection to true learning objectives? Are they focused? Student responses provide an indication of how well teachers communicate learning goals and whether students are engaged and intentional about their learning.

Continued on next page ❯

Try This: Using Classroom Walkthroughs to Reduce Variance in Teaching Quality (continued)

Are students learning both basic and higher-order levels of knowledge? Ideally, students should be learning at not just the lower levels of Bloom's taxonomy (remembering, understanding, and applying) but also the higher levels of analyzing, evaluating, and creating. If principals observe that student learning is consistently concentrated on lower levels, they should work with teachers to incorporate higher-order learning activities into their lesson plans.

Do student achievement data correlate with walkthrough data? Finally, principals should observe classrooms through the lens of student achievement data. Are teachers using different strategies in classrooms where students perform at higher levels? What effective strategies might be imported from one classroom to another?

One or two observations won't reveal much, but 10 visits to 40 classrooms will. Think of walkthroughs as tiles in a mosaic: One tile in isolation tells almost nothing, but when 400 tiles are laid out in an orderly manner, a picture emerges—in this case, one that can guide a school to better teaching and higher levels of student achievement.

Source: Adapted from "Classroom Observations: Learning to See the Forest *and* the Trees," by H. Pitler with B. Goodwin, Summer 2008, *Changing Schools, 58,* 19–21.

To stem the rising tide of crime, the city decided to focus on fixing a handful of little things. They were guided by Broken Windows theory, which states, in a nutshell, that when a window is left broken in a building, it sends the message to passersby that "no one cares and no one is in charge" (p. 141). Soon, more broken windows appear, and, eventually, the whole neighborhood descends into chaos.

Against the advice of those who said the city should focus on "bigger" questions of crime and making sure the subway trains ran on time, New York spent its energies (and dollars) painting over the graffiti on subway cars, cracking down on "fare beating" (people jumping over turnstiles to avoid paying fares), and ejecting people from stations for drunkenness or bad behavior. By the early 1990s, the murder rate in the Big Apple had fallen by two-thirds; felonies were cut in half citywide and by three-quarters in the subway system. As Gladwell observes, sometimes big problems "can be reversed, can be tipped, by tinkering with the smallest details of the immediate environment" (p. 146).

The same theory may apply to school performance. Even innovations and influences with relatively small effect sizes may still be worth doing if they can be combined in mutually reinforcing or additive ways—that is, if leaders are clear about how some efforts that may have less individual impact on student achievement, such as setting a vision or creating opportunities for teacher collaboration, can add up to big improvements in school performance when they are thoughtfully integrated. This is what McREL discovered during a four-year study of schools that beat the odds by helping all students, including at-risk students, achieve at high academic levels.

In 2001, McREL researchers set out to determine how high-poverty, high-performing, beat-the-odds schools differ from low-performing schools (McREL, 2005b). They identified 739 high-performing and 738 low-performing schools with 50 percent or more of their students eligible for free and reduced-price lunch. Teachers in those schools were surveyed about their schools' performance in four key areas— (1) school environment, (2) professional community, (3) leadership, and (4) instruction— and were asked to agree or disagree with statements such as these:

- My school has an explicit statement of high expectations concerning student achievement.

- There is a safe, orderly learning environment in my school.

- Administrators, teachers, and parents share a common vision of school improvement.

- My students know their learning goals.

Several differences emerged between the perceptions of teachers in high-performing schools and those in low-performing schools. Teachers in the low-performing schools reported that their schools appeared to be doing many of the "right" things that research says are correlated with higher levels of student achievement. For example, they were focusing on offering challenging curricula, encouraging teacher collaboration, and improving teachers' practices through high-quality professional development.

The missing ingredient—the thing that beat-the-odds schools were attending to that struggling schools were not—was their school culture. The beat-the-odds schools appeared to have aggregated many smaller influences together to create what we might call a "culture of high expectations." Individually, each of these influences (see Figure 4.2) is, at best, only moderately correlated with student achievement. When taken together, though, they appear to reinforce one another, creating a significant, positive effect on student achievement. Specifically, the beat-the-odds schools appear to develop, with input from teachers, a vision of success and a clear focus for their improvement efforts. This vision, in turn, sets high expectations for student performance *and* behavior.

That such well-worn school reform components as assessment and monitoring, collaboration, professional development, and individualizing instruction didn't surface as distinguishing features in McREL's examination of beat-the-odds schools doesn't mean they're unimportant. Indeed, teachers in high-performing schools reported that these things *were* being addressed in their schools, as did teachers in low-performing schools. In other words, these things weren't the *distinguishing* features of higher-performing schools. They appear to be necessary, but not sufficient, ingredients of reform. To make the leap from low- to high-performing, schools must transform their cultures— not only in terms of the kind of learning environment they create for students but also in the work environment they foster among the staff, volunteers, and parents. In short, the high-performing schools that McREL studied appear to create something akin to the "work hard, be nice" slogan that serves as the guiding principle for the Knowledge Is Power Program (KIPP) schools.

Figure 4.2
Distinguishing Characteristics of High-Performing, High-Needs Schools

Shared mission and goals (common vision and clear focus for resources)
Academic press for achievement (high expectations for all)
Orderly climate (clear and enforced rules for student behavior)
Support for teacher influence (leadership shared with teachers)
Structure (clear student goals, strong classroom management)

The "Work Hard, Be Nice" Culture in KIPP Schools

According to Jay Mathews's book *Work Hard, Be Nice: How Two Inspired Teachers Created the Most Promising Schools in America* (2009), when KIPP founders Michael Feinberg and David Levin first pitched their reform model to officials in Houston, Texas, the first question they often received was, "So what new curriculum are you using?"

"Well, you know, there isn't going to be any new curriculum," Levin and Feinberg would respond. The district, in their view, had already designed a good curriculum. "We just want to make sure the kids learn it" (p. 7).

This response brought puzzled looks from administrators, who, at that time, were apt to equate reform *with* new approaches to curriculum. The "special sauce" of KIPP, however, is not a new or different kind of curriculum; rather, it's a no-nonsense, direct approach to instruction combined with an obsessive insistence on creating cultures of high performance and expectations.

The KIPP approach was inspired by Harriet Ball, a veteran of inner-city schools who mentored Levin and Feinberg when they were novice teachers. In KIPP classrooms, children often chant in unison to learn, for example, factors of nine (e.g., "nine, eighteen, twenty-seven, thirty-six"). However, the chants aren't the *only* method of instruction; rather, they're "disposable crutches"— something similar to scaffolded learning, used to help children memorize important content or motivate them to learn. Both Levin and Feinberg gained a reputation for being rigid (if not overbearing) taskmasters when it came to instruction. A constant presence in teachers' classrooms, they did not hesitate to interfere or even reteach a lesson if they felt teachers had taught something poorly. When hiring new teachers, they carefully scrutinized them to ensure that they were "on the same wavelength" as Levin and Feinberg—in terms of how they taught as well as their belief that all children not only *can* learn but "*will* learn" (p. 37).

To create a culture of high expectations for learning and behavior in their schools, Levin and Feinberg developed a four-part credo:

1. "Work hard, be nice";

2. "There are no shortcuts" (a phrase borrowed from celebrated teacher Rafe Esquith);

3. "Assign yourself" (that is, students are to take personal responsibility for their own learning); and

4. "If there is a problem, we look for a solution. If there is a better way, we find it. If a team member needs help, we give it. If we need help, we ask" (p. 179).

This credo is intended to be more than just wall art. All KIPP students, parents, and teachers must sign written agreements committing to it—for example, students agree to do their homework (about two hours each night), parents commit to getting their children to school on time and dressed properly, and teachers commit to making themselves available every weeknight to answer student phone calls and questions about homework.

In their own take on the Broken Windows theory, both Feinberg and Levin were obsessed with nearly every working detail of their schools—right down to classroom bulletin boards. They were known to enter teachers' classrooms at night and fix the boards, straightening pictures or lettering to ensure that they "radiated excitement" for learning and striving to be the best (p. 176).

Levin and Feinberg also insisted on high standards of student behavior in the school. Even the slightest infraction—for example, not turning in homework, or making fun of other students—could bring swift retribution. As punishment, students were often sentenced to "the Porch" (an allusion to the adage, "If you can't run with the big dogs, sit on the porch"), where they might go a day or even a week forbidden to speak to anyone except the teacher until they demonstrated improved behavior or effort.

"As teachers," Mathews writes, Levin and Feinberg "tried to draw lines that could not be crossed" (p. 213). The purpose of these rigid structures was not to humiliate or punish students but, rather, to ensure that the school offered them a safe haven—a place where everyone could feel free from bullies and the anxieties of the uncertain environments outside the walls of the school. In short, behind Levin and Feinberg's obsession with school culture was the desire to make KIPP "an island of peace" in its students' otherwise chaotic lives (p. 214).

Low-Performing Schools: One Big, Unhappy Family

Tolstoy's *Anna Karenina* famously opens with the line "Happy families are all alike; every unhappy family is unhappy in its own way." School cultures are no different. While high-functioning schools reflect many similar characteristics, low-performing schools display an array of dysfunctional behaviors. In his book *So Much Reform, So Little Change* (2008), Charles Payne provides numerous examples of toxic, dysfunctional school cultures. One such example is the story of Jacqueline Kingon, a teacher in a high-poverty school in the Bronx that, by all counts, was in the middle of a figurative spin stall. In a 2001 *New York Times* article, Kingon (2001) described her experience at the school as follows.

During her first day at the school, Kingon feels as if she's entered the "Twilight Zone" when she notices that none of the wall clocks are set to the same time. A veteran teacher advises her to "work around it" by wearing a watch. When she finds the school's custodian, he reports that he sent requests to the district office to repair the clocks, but it was so long ago that the copy of the requisition he sent has faded from blue to white.

On the first floor of the building, Kingon discovers a "graveyard" of textbooks no longer aligned with the school's new reading program. Veteran teachers ruefully predict that the new program will probably be changed again after two or three years, just as everyone starts to get comfortable with it, because of its inevitable lack of results.

In the faculty lounge, she asks for advice on managing her classroom. One veteran teacher offers this technique: "I scream in their ear." Another adds, "I scream in their *face*." Others tell her that "[busy] work that makes students comfortable and feel successful causes fewer discipline problems." They try to convince her that "dumbing down is a discipline technique that keeps children who prefer entertainment to instruction orderly and safe."

Kingon finds that dealing with disruptive students requires a six-step discipline process that reads like something out of a Franz Kafka novel. She must write up students several times, meet with their parents, endure a 7- to 10-day cooling-off period, draft a report to the guidance counselors—all before ever notifying the principal of the problem.

The other teachers in the school lack the time and energy to complete the process. When Kingon attempts to follow the process, she learns that writing too many reports (including three about a boy who tried to suffocate himself with a plastic bag and throw himself from a third-story window) results in a sharp reprimand from the principal for losing control of her classroom. He gives her two weeks to "shape up or ship out." Eventually, she capitulates, learning to keep her head down and her disciplinary reports to the bare minimum required to, per the advice she heard repeatedly from veteran teachers, "cover" herself.

Sadly, Kingon's experience is all too common—especially the lack of trust and the need to "cover" herself, which Payne notes is often the heart of the problem in low-performing schools. He cites ongoing research from the

Consortium on Chicago School Research to support this perspective. When the consortium compared the 30 most highly rated schools in Chicago with 30 of the lowest-performing schools, its researchers discovered that questions related to the quality of relationships—in particular, the level of trust and respect teachers have for one another—proved to be one of the best predictors of school performance (Payne, 2008, p. 37).

The Power of "Can Do"

In his book *Learned Optimism: How to Change Your Mind and Your Life* (1990), Martin Seligman recounts the unintended outcomes of a laboratory experiment conducted at the University of Pennsylvania in the mid-1960s. The purpose of the experiment was to see if dogs would become conditioned to a particular tone when it was followed by a mild electrical shock (akin to a static shock) and exhibit a Pavlovian response, reacting with fear when they heard the tone.

After conditioning the dogs to the pairing of the tone with the shock, the researchers placed the dogs into a large box with two compartments separated by a low wall that the dogs could easily jump over. The scientists expected that when they rang the tone, the dogs would jump into the next compartment to avoid the coming shock. Instead, the dogs cowered and whimpered, making no attempt to avoid the coming jolts of electricity.

Seligman realized that the dogs had been "taught" to be helpless. During the conditioning, nothing they did changed the outcome (they got shocked every time); thus, they "learned that nothing they did mattered. So why try?" (p. 20). Observing the dogs' "learned helplessness," Seligman realized that downtrodden people often exhibit similar behavior. He thus began a 20-year quest to determine how one's prevailing outlook on life, whether optimistic or pessimistic, can lead to dramatically different life choices and outcomes.

In many ways, the cultures of low-performing schools reflect a similar kind of learned helplessness. Teachers in these schools come to believe that nothing ever gets better and nothing they do matters, so they hunker down and wait for each new program to pass as quickly as possible. In such demoralized school cultures, technical fixes—such as bringing in a new reading program, creating 90-minute reading blocks, or extending the school day—rarely have much impact.

In contrast, teachers in high-performing schools believe that success is possible; they believe that as individuals and as a group, they are capable of improving student achievement. And they trust their colleagues to work as hard as they do to make it happen. Hoy, Tarter, and Hoy (2006) coined the term *academic optimism* as a way to define the cultures of high-performing schools that display the following characteristics:

- Press for academic achievement

- Collective efficacy (i.e., a shared belief among teachers that they can help students succeed)

- Faculty trust in parents and students

After surveying teachers in nearly 100 schools, Hoy and colleagues determined that academic optimism was an even more powerful predictor of student achievement than students' socioeconomic status:

> In the same way individuals can develop learned helplessness, organizations can be seduced by pervasive pessimism. According to the pessimist view, voiced with a tired resignation, "These kids can't learn, and there is nothing I can do about it, so why worry about academic achievement...." Academic optimism, in stark contrast, views teachers as capable, students as willing, parents as supportive, and the task as achievable. (p. 440)

A McREL meta-analysis of research on effective leaders similarly points to the importance of building a "can-do" school culture (Marzano et al., 2005). Most notably, among 21 responsibilities of school leaders linked to higher levels of student achievement, the study found that effective principals

- Set high, concrete goals and expectations for all students to reach those goals.

- Develop a clear vision for what the school could be like and promote a sense of staff cooperation and cohesion.

- Involve teachers in decision making and shared leadership.

- Systematically celebrate teachers' accomplishments.

For some, focusing on something as amorphous as organizational culture may seem hopelessly touchy-feely. Consider, though, that former General Electric CEO Jack Welch, who could hardly be accused of touchy-feely management practices, identified building a strong corporate culture as one of the two main duties of any CEO, with the other duty being to develop leaders. Maintaining a strong company culture was so important to Welch that he passed over many seemingly good merger deals due to his concerns about cultural fit (Welch & Welch, 2005).

Research on School Turnarounds

Now that we have a pretty good sense of what high-performing schools look and feel like, the question remains: What process did they use to transform themselves from dysfunctional schools into stellar ones?

Unfortunately, research can only offer limited answers to this question. While a great deal of research exists on what good schools do that low-performing ones don't, there's not a lot of data on what struggling schools do to *become* effective ones. At this point, what we do know about school turnaround generally comes from qualitative research—that is, case studies or expert opinion based on field experience. A few years ago, the nonprofit Public Impact (2007) summarized this body of research, as well as studies of turnarounds in other public- and private-sector institutions. Following are the elements that Public Impact found were most important to successful institutional improvement efforts.

Focus

Very few, if any, examples exist of schools or districts that tried to "do it all" at once and succeeded. Indeed, most "systemic" reforms usually result in people doing too much and accomplishing too little. As Payne (2008) notes, when used in conversations about school reform, the word *systemic* really appears to mean, "Let's pretend to do on a grand scale what we have no idea how to do on a small scale" (p. 169).

That's not to say that continuous improvement efforts shouldn't eventually address many factors, such as the five components of the What Matters Most framework discussed in the introduction to this book. It's that doing things right takes time, focus, and effort, so it's important to keep improvement efforts focused and manageable. A useful reminder here may be "Hofstadter's Law," the tongue-in-cheek principle coined by Douglas Hofstadter (1979):

"It always takes longer than you expect, even when you take into account Hofstadter's Law" (p. 152).

Speed

Effective turnaround efforts are "fast"—that is, they are designed to demonstrate tangible results within a few months. The idea is to convey to students, staff, parents, and everyone involved with the school that things are changing, right now, for the better in some very real and substantive ways.

Planning

School leaders should not simply shoot from the hip, just to impress everyone that "something's being done." To the contrary, the Public Impact study found that the most successful turnaround efforts were in planning for several months to a full year before being implemented, while those that had been in planning for fewer than three months tended to be less effective.

Freedom

Often, the rules and structures that are in place—for example, hiring procedures and resource allocation—are part of the reason for a school's low performance. Struggling schools usually need to make big, substantive changes and are not likely to make those changes if they remain strait-jacketed by existing structures. Thus, most successful turnarounds appear to have been given some freedom from rules and regulations by the governing bodies—or alternatively, had a strong leader who adopted an "act now and ask forgiveness later" approach to improvement. An important caveat here is that, by itself, simply giving a struggling school more autonomy is not likely to improve its performance; other variables of accountability and support must also be in place.

Support

Most successful turnarounds appear to have had the ongoing support of a governing body that offered guidance but did not micromanage or insist on approving, item by item, everything the school was doing.

Community Engagement

Successful turnarounds engage their surrounding communities at appropriate times, to create a shared sense of urgency and need for the change as well as to seek input from teachers, students, and parents to ensure that the changes are responsive to the needs of the community. The idea is to encourage stakeholders to "get on stage" with the rest of the performers in the process instead of just becoming "peanut gallery" critics.

Leadership

There's little question that turnarounds require a strong, insightful, and persuasive leader at the helm. Research also suggests that a leader who may be incredibly effective at maintaining a well-functioning organization may lack the stomach, insight, or skills to be effective in turning around a school—and vice versa. As Marzano, Waters, and McNulty (2005) note, leaders appear to emphasize a different set of responsibilities when leading "second-order" changes—that is, broad, sweeping changes that take people out of the comfort zones of their existing know-how and cause them to reexamine their values and beliefs.

When leading second-order changes, leaders must serve as catalysts for change, shaking up the status quo and articulating a new vision for the school. That said, they must also be aware of and attentive to the fact that change is never easy for people. They must keep the lines of communication open, listen to what people are going through, help them reexamine their own attitudes and beliefs, and make sure they have the training or resources needed to do what's expected of them.

Using Focus and Quick Wins to Transform Culture: One School's Story

So what does an effective turnaround effort look like in real life? Here's a story of one school that took a focused approach to transform its culture and dramatically raise student achievement.

In 2001, when the staff of Alcester-Hudson elementary school in South Dakota first learned that the state had designated the school "in need of improvement," they felt the same mix of emotions people experience upon the death of a beloved family member—denial, anger, grief, and uncertainty about what to do next.

"Looking back, going on school improvement status was the best thing that ever happened to us," said Elementary School coordinator Kathy Johannsen. "But at the time, we were surprised, embarrassed, and humiliated. We always thought of our school as a good school, one that met the needs of our students and community. To be publicly labeled as 'unsatisfactory' was just horrible" (Galvin & Parsley, 2005).

Three years after beginning their improvement efforts, though, the staff at Alcester-Hudson had solved their own problems. Student achievement rose dramatically—94 percent of students tested proficient on the state math test and 100 percent of students tested proficient in reading. The school that was once in "need of improvement" received the state's highest rating: "commendable."

Several keys to success emerge from Alcester's story.

Distributing Leadership

Much like a barn raising, school improvement is too big of a job for any single person to handle. A school can improve only with widespread commitment to the effort and many people involved in planning and carrying it out. With this in mind, from the outset, the staff at Alcester-Hudson Elementary formed a leadership team to manage the steps of the improvement process, beginning with writing the school improvement plan.

Cheryl Johnson, a school board representative on the team, commented on the leadership changes she observed over time. "I remember going to the first meeting and it was just helter skelter—everyone trying to do his or her own thing and no one wanting to take charge. Now we have teachers volunteering to take on leadership roles in various areas. The great majority of the teachers at Alcester Hudson Elementary are very comfortable being leaders and taking the initiative to begin new projects."

Getting on the Same Page

Like teachers at many schools, those at Alcester-Hudson Elementary were almost entirely autonomous in the beginning—they tended to close their classroom doors each morning and do their own thing during the day. McREL consultants working in the school noticed right away that their math program was being implemented differently in each classroom and that there were differing levels of expectation in reading from room to room. They encouraged school staff members to take a "balcony view"—to step back and look at themselves with a new eye. With some coaching, the faculty began to see how many aspects of their school culture, including the autonomy of their teachers, left them with little sense that they could work together to make a difference.

They also began to take a hard look at their student achievement data and developed a number of "shared agreements," including teaching mathematics for an hour and 15 minutes per day, following timelines for completing various portions of the math curriculum, implementing a rigorous schedule of both formative and summative assessments in reading and math, and using new guided reading strategies in grades K–3.

Getting Hooked on Data

Early on in the improvement process, the entire faculty of the school began to dig into their data to "confront brutal facts" (to borrow a phrase from Jim Collins) about how students were performing as well as to speculate on what might contribute to these results. Everyone on staff learned the cycle of school improvement: study data, form hypotheses, plan and implement changes in instruction, reallocate resources, and measure changes in student learning.

The teachers at Alcester-Hudson grew so adept at using data that, just as successful students are able to anticipate how they've done on a test before seeing the results, they were able to use formative assessments to predict each student's learning in relation to the state and district content standards. When asked to predict how well students would do on the upcoming state tests in 2002, teachers agreed that scores would decline because they realized that they had let up on their efforts. Their predictions were accurate: achievement scores dipped. The chagrined staff quickly recommitted to keeping up the efforts that had led to their initial success.

At the same time, data became a vehicle for noting success and celebrating the achievements of the staff. Today, everything in the school revolves around data. As school leadership team member Kathy Johannsen related, she has been "totally converted … into a data junkie. Now with many of our challenges or issues that come up, my first thought is, 'We need to gather data.' I had never thought about that before—how important data can be and how many kinds of data you can collect for so many different reasons."

Staying Focused (Taking It One Step at a Time)

Too often, data can leave educators feeling overwhelmed and discouraged, knowing that they have much need for improvement but unsure where to begin—a bit like trying to clean the home of a compulsive hoarder. At Alcester-Hudson, the leadership team staff learned the importance of using the data to focus on one problem at a time. For example, they initially identified specific numerical achievement targets in reading and mathematics. After a year of consistent focus on instructional goals and discussions around student achievement, the teachers were gratified (but not surprised) to see test scores rise significantly on the yearly summative assessments given by the state. In fact, all students (including special education students) met the school's goals. With these "quick wins" under their belts, staff consulted the data again and identified a new, research-based focus for their improvement efforts.

Looking to Research for Answers

Once the staff knew what direction to take, they turned to rigorous research to learn effective strategies that would help them achieve their shared goals. The teachers drew from a variety of sources for this information—including research from the books *Classroom Instruction that Works* (Marzano et al., 2001) and *What Works in Schools* (Marzano, 2003) and from their local Special Education Co-op, as well as professional wisdom and lessons learned from peers in neighboring schools.

Creating a Community of Professionals

During initial discussions about reallocating resources to support their improvement goals, the teachers at Alcester-Hudson developed a scheduling strategy that allowed them to meet monthly in instructional teams (K–3 and 4–6) on what they called "Working Wednesdays." During this two-hour, uninterrupted block of time, classroom, special education, and Title I teachers met together to discuss instructional strategies and the needs of individual children not meeting the standards. They drew up lists of students, posted them, and saved them from week to week.

These Working Wednesday discussions made teachers more aware of their own attitudes about student learning. As teachers learned about strategies others were using, they gained an increased awareness of the learning potential of all students. They would share strategies and propose new ideas to get students "off the list." Soon, the conversations turned to what changes teachers could make in their instruction, and they began to celebrate together when data revealed they could remove a student from the list.

Turning Quick Wins into Lasting Changes

The Alcester-Hudson staff's original perception of the improvement process as a "way to get off improvement" quickly evolved to something very different as they began to experience success. Bobette Anderson, a 4th grade teacher and an original member of the leadership team, said, "When we started working on school improvement it was because our test scores were not up to par for two years. When we started the process, we were trying to fix things in a hurry. As we got to working, we realized there was more to improvement than just fixing your immediate problems, and it was going to take some work."

Kathy Johannsen added, "I knew that we were a school marked for improvement by the state and that we needed to improve our standardized test scores. But it's much, much more than that. The school improvement process is just what it says it is—it improves a lot more than just your test scores. It improves literally every aspect of the school—how we interact with each other as staff members, how we work with kids, what we're teaching those kids, and what the climate of our school is."

In sum, although Alcester-Hudson kept its initial efforts focused and geared toward getting quick gains in test scores, the improvement process ultimately became a comprehensive effort. The takeaway from this story is that in order to be effective and sustainable, school improvement efforts need to, in the end, be broad and systemic but in the beginning, be focused and targeted on specific problems. Metaphorically speaking, what starts with fixing a few broken windows eventually becomes an effort to revitalize an entire school community.

Epilogue: Improvement Never Ends

Another member of the Alcester-Hudson leadership team, Mary Beth Lundberg, noted that after three years of school improvement, the school staff realized that despite a dramatic increase in student test scores, their work was far from over. "Once the job of improving your scores is over, the work continues. Before this whole process started I looked at where we had to go with our scores and thought, 'Okay, we'll get there, and then we'll be done.' Now my full belief is that we should never be done. We need to constantly look to improve, and even if we increase achievement every single year, we should pat ourselves on the back but then get back down to pulling apart the scores and looking for ways to improve" (McREL, n.d.). In 2010, Alcester-Hudson remained on South Dakota's list of distinguished schools with 93 percent of its students demonstrating proficiency in math and reading—and with 99 percent of its students demonstrating a basic or higher level of performance in both subjects.

Final Thoughts: Fractals and Touchstones

I opened this chapter drawing a parallel between the panic of early aviators who found themselves spinning perilously to the ground and educators in low-performing schools who may find themselves in a similar downward spiral, unable to right themselves despite countless—maybe even frantic—attempts to do so. Just as pilots have learned to recover from spins by doing less, not more, low-performing schools can likewise pull out of their spins and right themselves by focusing on doing a few simple things well.

One way for schools to adopt a less-is-more approach is to engage in what my colleagues at McREL have come to call a *fractal experience*—a small-scale, short-term effort that results in quick, measurable gains in achievement. The term *fractal* is drawn from a phenomenon found throughout nature in such things as ferns, snowflakes, and river networks, where the smallest component of the system resembles the larger system.

Try This: Getting Quick Wins with Fractal Experiences

Here are the simple steps a school can take to create a fractal experience.

- Select a time-bound, specific, measurable (and attainable) goal—for example, student absences from school and class will decrease 20 percent by the end of this trimester.

- Identify simple (ideally already existing) indicators for measuring progress.

- Secure specific commitments from everyone—from teachers to media specialists to front office staff to bus drivers—for what they will do to accomplish the goal.

- Monitor implementation of the effort—Is everyone doing what they committed to do?

- After the specified period, review what happened, attributing success or failure to the collective effort.

- Identify ways to sustain the successful change or to improve results during the next improvement cycle.

- If the experience is successful, identify a new "fractal"—that is, a way to build on the existing effort to increase its impact.

Here are some real examples of simple fractal experiences that initiated "bigger and better" continuous improvement efforts.

Continued on next page ❯

Schools can adopt small-scale, carefully designed school improvement experiences that contain the same elements as larger schoolwide improvement efforts (e.g., using data, setting goals, clarifying individual behaviors, and monitoring implementation). For example, educators at a high school that McREL consultants worked with in North Carolina determined after analyzing data that their school climate was a major concern and should be the initial focus of their improvement efforts. They further narrowed this focus to a simple problem: unruly behavior during passing time, which was creating a chaotic and sometimes unsafe environment.

As a first step to addressing this problem, school staff decided, collectively, that all teachers should spend the passing period standing in the doorway of their classrooms, monitoring student behavior, and greeting students as they entered the classroom. Because they knew the effort would work only if every teacher in the building took part in it and stuck with it, they established clear expectations and consistently monitored the implementation of the effort. After only a few weeks, they found that tardiness and unruly behavior declined and students arrived in class more ready to learn. As a result of this experience, they could feel the culture of their school beginning to change from one of pessimism to the kind of academic optimism discussed earlier in this chapter. Moreover, they were able to build on this positive experience and use the same process to engage in more comprehensive efforts to improve the climate and culture of the school.

Often, schoolwide improvement efforts bog down in implementation. In part, this is because those implementing the changes remain unconvinced that the efforts will pay off or because they lose faith in the effort when they do not see it bear fruit. In fractal experiences, schools implement small-scale improvement processes that generate quick wins—which, in turn, encourage those implementing the changes to take on larger challenges. Because fractals are small, simple, and completed in a short time, it's easier for stakeholders to "connect the dots" between actions taken and outcomes produced. Moreover, the quick wins help to create a can-do attitude or a sense of academic optimism, which is a key predictor of school success. Quick wins encourage school staff members to undertake ever more complex and substantive improvement efforts, which have the dramatic effect of transforming the school's culture.

Rather than trying to do many things and doing none of them well, schools can identify one or two big things to do next, while recognizing that often what needs to change most is their own school culture. By paying attention to improving teaching and learning, as well as transforming their climate and culture, schools eventually find that their improvement efforts have become comprehensive and systemic. Schools that take this measured approach recover from spin stalls and find themselves on an upward ascent of improved attitudes, increasing optimism, and rising student performance.

The Touchstones

Research suggests the following touchstones as the key to creating high-performance school cultures:

Improving the quality and reducing the variance of teaching quality in the school. Researchers have observed significant variance in the quality of instruction provided to students *within the same school*. At the same time, leadership behaviors that focus on developing teachers appear to be much more powerful than those that focus on developing the organization. Thus, leaders would do well to focus attention and energies on improving classroom instruction.

Try This: Getting Quick Wins with Fractal Experiences (continued)

- To improve the English language acquisition of immigrant students, an elementary school in Jefferson County, Colorado, got everyone in the school involved in encouraging these students to extend their verbal answers from one word to many. Even cafeteria workers asked for extended responses from students as they went through the lines.

- To increase the involvement of parents whose children were struggling in school, teachers in a North Carolina elementary school made personal phone calls to parents who had previously skipped parent–teacher conferences. The gentle reminders resulted in much higher parent participation in the conferences and helped teachers and parents work together to help students succeed.

Source: Adapted from "'Fractal' Experiences, Quick Wins, and School Successes," M. Galvin, Spring 2007, *Changing Schools, 55,* 10.

High-Performance School Cultures: A Sample Checklist

Raising the quality and reducing the variability of teaching across the school

☐ Expectations for instruction are clearly and consistently articulated across the school.

☐ Principals/instructional leaders conduct regular classroom observations with follow-up coaching conversations.

☐ Teachers engage in professional conversations that focus on improving instructional practice.

Creating a culture of high expectations for academics and behavior

☐ High expectations for learning and behavior are clearly articulated and enforced.

☐ In keeping with the Broken Windows theory, the physical appearance of the school conveys high expectations for student learning.

☐ All school personnel—from teachers to support and janitorial staff—can connect their work to student success.

Creating a culture of high expectations for academics and behavior. Improving instruction may be difficult to do in a dysfunctional school. It may even feel like tilting at windmills in an otherwise chaotic, disorderly environment. Thus, school leaders must also work to create high-performance cultures within the school that promote a "work hard, be nice" learning environment for students as well as a "can-do" attitude among adults.

5

Developing High-Reliability District Systems

On September 29, 2007, British Airways Flight 55 was approximately 37,000 feet above Marseilles, France, two hours into an 11-hour jaunt to Johannesburg, South Africa. In all, 310 souls were on board the 747, including passengers and crew. Beneath them on the ground, air controllers in Marseilles had directed an Aerolinas Argentinas flight en route from Rome to Buenos Aires to climb to the same altitude, over the same stretch of Mediterranean coastline. What happened next was reportedly "hushed up" by airline officials (Massey, 2007).

A decade before, Britain's Civil Aviation Authority had put off repeated requests from pilots and others to mandate the use of Traffic Collision Avoidance Systems (TCAS) on all British aircraft, which would warn pilots if they were on a collision course with other planes. At the time, authorities had argued that the expensive system (around $200,000 per plane) would cause too many false alarms and implementation would take years to coordinate with other European agencies (Wolmar, 1994).

According to later reports of the incident in the skies over Marseilles, passengers in the rear of the British aircraft were the first to see the Argentine plane approaching. They began screaming frantically as the Airbus, which had likely reached its typical cruising speed of 537 mph, rapidly closed the distance on the British plane.

Here's where our story takes an unexpected turn.

Despite the high costs and initial bureaucratic foot dragging, the British Airways plane, like all aircraft in the BA fleet, *had* been fitted with a TCAS. As the Argentine plane came within a few thousand feet of the British jet, an alarm went off in the cockpit of the aircraft, giving the pilot a loud and insistent command to "climb, climb, climb." The captain took the controls and pointed the nose of the aircraft upward, climbing steeply and banking to the right, narrowly avoiding the other plane. What could have been a tragic disaster was averted by a fail-safe warning system aboard the British aircraft and a well-trained pilot who knew what to do when the warning sounded.

Plenty of other safety systems and processes were in place on the ground. Air-traffic controllers had access to radar screens that indicated the location of aircraft and, of course, were not supposed to put two planes on the same flight path. The pilots had been trained to be vigilant, scanning the skies for other planes. Yet these systems and processes all failed to identify the approaching disaster.

For high-reliability organizations—such as airlines, nuclear power plants, and oil refineries—any mistake can have disastrous consequences. Thus, they put into place multilayered systems to prevent errors and develop standard procedures to respond quickly when alarms do sound. These high-reliability or fail-safe systems are characterized by a clear commitment to error-free performance (no airline aims for anything less than 100 percent of its planes landing safely); standardized routines and expectations to ensure error-free, day-to-day performance; and, finally, a healthy obsession with failure (continually looking for ways to address error patterns).

Modeling school systems after high-reliability organizations is the last key to changing the odds for students. This final component of the What Matters Most framework is not so much a new or additional leverage point, but rather a way of thinking about how to bring together and leverage the other four high-impact areas of the framework by ensuring their flawless implementation. In other words, the simple and straightforward idea at the heart of this final area of the framework is this: One of the most powerful things school systems can do to change the odds for all students is simply doing *well* what they already know they must do.

The Surprising Success of "Vanilla" Reforms

In the summer of 1989, Sam Stringfield, a professor and researcher at Johns Hopkins University, stumbled across a mystery. Along with a colleague, Charles Teddlie, he had been staring at a "mountain of data" gathered through the Louisiana School Effectiveness Study, an examination of eight pairs of matched schools of similar size and demographics in which one member of the pair was striking in its high performance and the other striking in its low performance.

A team of observers had gone to all 16 elementary schools to gather qualitative data that the researchers hoped would tease out the differences between their approaches. In true "double-blind" research fashion, the observers were not told which schools were the positive or negative outliers. And yet, to a person, they had all been able to discern—without the benefit of seeing any student performance data—the high performers from the low performers.

Stringfield spent the summer sifting through the observers' case studies, trying to figure out how these people, most of whom were not professional educators, had so easily sorted out the princes from the frogs. The low-performing schools weren't *obviously* horrible. Each had a star teacher or two; they tended to have several programs in place and other seemingly positive things happening to commend them. On the other hand, the top-performing schools were, to be frank, a little boring. Some were grossly underfunded. None were implementing the latest reform du jour. "In fact," as Stringfield later recalled, "several were as plain vanilla schools as could be imagined" (Stringfield, Reynolds, & Schaffer, 2010, p. 14).

Avoiding the "Box of Chocolates" Effect

There was, however, one striking difference between the two sets of schools, which the observers appeared to have picked up on. In the low-performing schools, an "anything goes" attitude appeared to prevail, with a wide range of teacher and student behaviors being tolerated. In contrast, the high-performing schools had a much clearer focus on student achievement and maintained much more consistent standards of teacher and student behavior.

In a word, the high-performing schools were more reliable. Observers could walk into different classrooms in these schools and see the same thing occurring: good teaching. Classrooms in the low-performing schools, on the other hand, were more like Forrest Gump's box of chocolates: you never knew what you were going to get.

From these observations, Stringfield concluded that schools—and by extension, school districts—don't need to be flashy or up on all the latest trends to be effective. They just need to ensure that students receive the same high-quality learning experiences in every classroom and in every school. While pondering these things, he came across an article in the *Smithsonian* magazine that discussed high-reliability organizations.

A New Way of Thinking About Schools

Stringfield started to wonder if perhaps high-performing schools and districts might have something in common with these high-reliability organizations. He began to outline several "HRO principles" that might be applied to schools. These principles included establishing and communicating clear goals, training and evaluating teaching staff to ensure optimal performance, and being preoccupied with identifying and correcting failures in student performance. Stringfield began to pull these ideas together into a new way of thinking about schools and districts as high-reliability organizations. At first, his ideas were purely theoretical. Yet over the years, other researchers and new studies began to confirm these principles—finding strong links between their presence in schools and districts and higher levels of student achievement.

Setting Clear, "No Excuses" Goals

Since the early 1970s, many researchers have surveyed districts on a variety of factors, looking for those with the strongest relationship to student achievement. In 2006, McREL pulled these studies—27 in all—together into a meta-analysis that examined the relationship between key superintendent leadership behaviors and student achievement (Waters & Marzano, 2006). One of the most prominent findings from this study (and perhaps the most reassuring to district administrators) was that overall, a statistically significant relationship (a positive correlation [r] of .24, which converts to d = .51) exists between ratings of district leadership–related variables and student achievement. Furthermore, the study found that five key leadership responsibilities were significantly tied to student achievement. All five (and their associated practices) relate directly to setting and keeping districts focused on districtwide goals for teaching and learning. They are as follows:

1. Engaging in collaborative goal-setting

2. Establishing nonnegotiable goals for achievement and instruction

3. Ensuring board alignment with and support of district goals

4. Monitoring goals for achievement and instruction

5. Using resources to support goals for instruction and achievement

Goal-setting, of course, is nothing new for districts. Most districts and schools are required to have improvement plans in place. Yet, if you were to walk into a typical school district and quiz staff members on their district's stated goals for student performance or the plans to raise achievement, how many would be able to recite them? Most likely, very few.

That's probably because many district improvement plans are excessively complicated. People seem to think, "Well, school improvement is not simple; therefore, the district goals and objectives reflect this complexity." Following this logic, Wells Fargo and Southwest Airlines should have multitiered goals and objectives with dizzyingly complicated improvement plans stored in hefty binders. Wells Fargo, for example, has 160,000 employees working in 6,000 banks across the United States, providing six different kinds of financial services. Southwest Airlines has 34,000 employees, who operate 3,400 daily flights, carrying 280,000 passengers out of 64 cities on 535 airplanes. Both are sprawling companies, operating in highly competitive and complex businesses. Yet, observers agree, one of their core strengths is their simplicity and clarity of focus.

"At the end of the day, they've kept it [their strategy] simple: generating more business out of existing customers," a banking analyst said of Wells Fargo to the *San Francisco Chronicle* (Temple, 2008, C-1). "What we did was so simple, and we kept it simple," a former Wells Fargo CEO told Jim Collins (2001). "It was so straightforward and obvious that it sounds almost ridiculous to talk about it" (p. 97).

Research points schools and districts to the same clarity of focus. As noted elsewhere in this book, researcher Robert Pianta found considerable variance in the learning experiences of students—even students in the same school. Overall, students have only about a 20 percent chance of receiving high-quality instruction throughout their elementary years. These data suggest that schools and districts could do worse than to narrow their focus to simply *guaranteeing* that all students, no matter the classroom where they find themselves, receive a world-class education from a supportive, highly effective teacher.

Attending to the Core Business: Great Teachers and Teaching

In 2007, McKinsey & Company studied the top-performing school systems in the world to determine what they are doing that others are not. Among the more striking findings from their analysis are their observations about what does *not* appear to make a difference:

- **More money**—Singapore spends less per pupil than most countries, yet it is among the top performers.

- **Extended school days**—Finnish students begin school later and study fewer hours, yet Finland ranks fourth among the top 10 school systems.

- **Smaller, autonomous schools**—Based on the idea that smaller was better, the Gates Foundation poured money into U.S. schools, only to discover that other factors outweighed school size and freedom.

What *does* work, according to the McKinsey & Company report, is

- Getting the right people to become teachers.

- Developing teachers into highly effective instructors.

- Tracking student performance and providing targeted support for struggling students.

As noted in the previous chapter, one touchstone for school leaders is to ensure high quality and low variability in the instruction provided to every child, in every classroom. At the *district* level, the corollary appears to be supporting high quality and low variability among *schools*. The McREL meta-analysis of effective district leadership practices noted earlier appears to confirm this observation: Nearly one-third (16 of 51) of the practices of effective district leaders identified in the meta-analysis relate to districts getting and keeping great teachers and supporting great teaching (see Figure 5.1).

Figure 5.1
Research-Based District Practices for Ensuring High-Quality Instruction in Every Classroom

1. **Hiring great teachers**

   - Screening, interviewing, and selecting teachers along with principals
   - Hiring experienced teachers
   - Directing personnel to ensure a stable yet improving and well-balanced workforce

2. **Adopting a flexible yet consistent approach to teaching**

   - Adopting nonnegotiable goals for achievement and instruction
   - Establishing agreement with the board president on the nature of teaching/learning strategies to be used in the district
   - Adopting instructional methodologies that facilitate efficient delivery of the district's curriculum
   - Incorporating varied and diverse instructional methodologies that allow for a wide range of learning styles that exist in a student population

3. **Supporting great teaching with individualized staff development**

   - Providing extensive teacher and principal staff development
   - Training all instructional staff in a common but flexible instructional model
   - Providing access to professional growth opportunities through the design of a master plan to coordinate in-service activities of the district
   - Adopting an instructional and resource management system supporting implementation of the district's instructional philosophy

4. **Ensuring great teaching through evaluation and accountability**

   - Using an instructional evaluation program that accurately monitors implementation of the district's instructional program
   - Tasking superintendents and district staff with observing classrooms during school visits
   - Establishing teacher evaluation as a priority for principals
   - Ensuring that principals speak with teachers about evaluation results
   - Rewarding successful teachers and terminating the employment of unsuccessful teachers

Source: Adapted from *School District Leadership that Works: The Effect of Superintendent Leadership on Student Achievement*, by J. T. Waters and R. J. Marzano, 2006, Denver, CO: McREL.

If we were to think of schools, at least for a moment, as businesses (an analogy with admitted limitations), we would identify its "core business" as teaching—just as a restaurant might view the heart of its business as the quality of its food. It only stands to reason, then, that district leaders should spent most of their time focusing on this core of their "business."

Creating Standard Operating Procedures

High-reliability organizations maintain high levels of consistency among their routine operations by first identifying and promulgating so-called standard operating procedures (SOPs). For school systems, SOPs might include developing districtwide curricula to ensure that students in school A get the same challenging content as students in school B. They might also require, as standard procedure, that all school leaders conduct walkthroughs and serve as instructional coaches. Basically, the idea is to identify ways in which variances might occur in the system that could leave some students receiving inferior learning experiences. In other words, just as the owner of a national restaurant chain seeks to guarantee that the Cobb salad served in the Toledo restaurant tastes just as fresh as the one served in Schenectady, district leaders should seek to guarantee the same high-quality learning experience for every student, no matter in what school or classroom he finds himself.

Hiring Great Teachers

Ensuring consistently good instruction, however, doesn't mean returning to the misguided attempts of yesteryear to create "teacher-proof" curricula that can be delivered by anyone. Rather, quite the opposite appears to be true. The most effective systems in the world, according to McKinsey & Company (2007), place the most capable teachers possible in classrooms by screening and interviewing qualified teachers and giving principals a stake in selecting them. If that sounds obvious, consider for a moment that according to an analysis of urban districts by the New Teacher Project, on average, roughly two-fifths of teachers are "forced placed" or transferred into a school with no input from principals. Moreover, many districts' drawn-out hiring processes cause districts to lose stronger candidates and hire weaker ones (Levin & Quinn, 2003).

Adopting a Consistent Yet Flexible Approach to Instruction

High-performing districts also develop master plans to coordinate staff development activities and train instructional staff in a shared but flexible approach to instruction. This doesn't mean that districts provide all teachers with scripted lessons. Rather, it means that they clearly define what good teaching looks like in classrooms in order to encourage a common instructional language across the district and ensure consistent use of research-based strategies in every classroom. For example, districts might set as an expectation that all students be taught using a Response to Intervention approach. They could also develop a list of sound instructional strategies that teachers should be using in the classroom and a template for lesson and unit plans. In addition, they might develop a shared protocol for classroom observations—that is, what principals or instructional leaders should look for in each classroom they visit and how often they should be visiting classrooms. These approaches would provide a broad framework for instruction that would ensure more consistency in teaching (overcoming the "box of chocolates" effect) while still allowing teachers the flexibility they need to adapt their teaching techniques to the needs of their students.

Supporting Great Teaching with Individualized Staff Development

Several other practices common to high-performing districts point to the importance of providing coordinated staff development efforts. As reported in a previous McREL synthesis of research, the most effective professional development focuses on improving teachers' classroom practices through modeling and coaching and improving teachers' subject-specific pedagogy (McREL, 2005a). Thus, as much as possible, districts should provide teachers with individualized, classroom-based professional development within a framework of a master staff-development plan.

Ensuring Great Teaching Through Evaluation and Accountability

As noted in the previous chapter, research makes a strong case for teachers to be regularly observed and evaluated. The district's role in this process is to ensure that principals regularly observe teachers and coach them to higher levels of performance. In addition, districts should ensure that principals fairly and consistently evaluate teachers in a way that promotes better teaching and professionalism.

Again, this may seem obvious, but it's far from standard practice. For example, a recent analysis of Colorado evaluation systems found that "nearly 100 percent of teachers in Colorado's largest school districts received satisfactory ratings in each of the past three years, an indication the state's system to improve classroom instruction is broken" (Mitchell, 2009). A similar nationwide examination of teacher evaluations conducted by the New Teacher Project in four states found that less than 1 percent of teachers were rated "unsatisfactory" (Weisberg, Sexton, Mulhern, & Keeling, 2009).

The Colorado study reported that "in a survey of nearly 900 Denver teachers, fewer than 40 percent agreed their evaluations were either accurate or helpful." Commenting on these results, Kim Ursetta, then head of the Denver teachers' union, noted that principals often wait until the end of the school year before hurriedly filling out evaluations of teachers. She lamented that "the evaluation is meant to be used as a tool for improving instruction, and instead we use it as a final exam" (Mitchell, 2009).

Let's put a finer point on these statistics and discuss the thorny topic of teacher terminations. Most would agree that even the best recruitment, goal-setting, staff development, and evaluation efforts will be undermined if persistently ineffective teachers remain in the classroom. In many urban districts, only a handful of teachers are terminated due to poor performance. For example, a 2007 study conducted by Research for Action of the School District of Philadelphia found that over the previous three years, on average, only four teachers out of 10,000 (less than one-tenth of 1 percent) had been terminated due to poor performance (Useem, Offenberg, & Farley, 2007). As Davis Guggenheim (2010) points out in his controversial film *Waiting for "Superman,"* over the course of their careers, approximately one in 57 doctors in Illinois lose their license to practice medicine, one in 97 lawyers lose their right to practice law, but only 1 in 2,500 teachers lose their right to teach.

Granted, as Diane Ravitch (2010) notes in her critique of the film, many other low-performing teachers are "counseled out" of their jobs, and nearly half leave the profession within five years. Nonetheless, it would appear that many others remain. For example, in a survey of principals and teachers, the New Teacher Project found that 81 percent of administrators and 58 percent of teachers say there is a tenured teacher in their school who is performing poorly (Weisberg et al., 2009).

For district leaders, teacher dismissal policies may feel like a political third rail. But according to a 2003 study by Public Agenda, nearly eight in 10 teachers agree that there are at least a few teachers in their building who are performing poorly (Farkas, Johnson, & Duffet, 2003). Moreover, nearly nine in 10 teachers say they would be open to or welcome their union's focusing more on evaluating teacher quality during collective bargaining. These data suggest that rank-and-file teachers, who may regularly inherit ill-prepared students, understand better than anyone the negative consequences of poor teaching and thus may be willing to meet district leaders halfway and openly discuss how to remove unproductive peers.

Maintaining a Healthy, Data-Driven Preoccupation with Failure

In his book *Better: A Surgeon's Notes on Performance* (2007), Atul Gawande describes how hospitals, where failures are often life-threatening, maintain a continual focus on the prevention of failure by implementing overlapping protocols to decrease the possibility of mistakes. The protocols are evident in Gawande's description of a typical surgery preparation to remove a cancerous growth:

> The operation was not going to be difficult or especially hazardous, but the team had to be meticulous about every step. On the day of surgery, before bringing her to the operating room, the anesthesiologist double-checked that it was safe to proceed. She reviewed [the patient's] medical history and medications, looked at her labs in the computer and at her EKG. She made sure that the patient had not had anything to eat for at least six hours and had her open her mouth to note any loose teeth that could fall out or dentures that should be removed. A nurse checked the patient's name band to make sure we had the right person; verified her drug allergies with her, confirmed that the procedure listed on her consent form was the one she expected. The nurse also looked for contact lenses that shouldn't be left in and for jewelry that could constrict a finger or snag on something. I made a mark with a felt-tip ten over the precise spot where [the patient] felt the lump, so there would be no mistaking the correct location. Early that morning before her surgery, [the patient] had also had a small amount of

radioactive tracer injected near her breast lump, in preparation for the sentinel lymph node biopsy. (p. 4)

The hospital staff follows several routine processes—some as simple as verifying the patient's identity and others as complex as the injection of a radioactive tracer—to reduce the risk of failure. Because error could be catastrophic, overlapping levels of checks and of responsibility ensure that any mistake that might slip through one level is caught by another. The system is by no means foolproof; we've all read horror stories of patients having the wrong limbs amputated or scalpels being left inside surgery patients. The point, though, is that hospitals have an organizational obsession with failure and make continuous efforts to avoid failing.

At first blush, schools may not appear to have much in common with hospitals or other high-reliability organizations such as nuclear power plants. And certainly, the failures of school systems are less dramatic—few newspaper headlines get written when a single student drops out of school. But while an individual child's academic failure may be less dramatic than a plane crash, nuclear meltdown, or death of a patient, they are tragic for that student. The question that Stringfield and others advocating for schools to model themselves after high-reliability organizations ask is this: What would school systems look like if they treated the failure of a single child with equal gravity as a nuclear meltdown or an airplane crash?

Warning Lights, Alarm Bells, and "Code Red" Procedures

Tom Bellamy, a professor at the University of Washington–Bothell who studies high-reliability organizations, has found that they recognize that systems will occasionally fail and problems will slip through (Bellamy, Crawford, Marshall, & Coulter, 2005). Thus, they have procedures in place so that once a problem is detected they can respond to it quickly. For example, a high truancy rate at a particular school might set off metaphorical alarm bells at the district office, which responds by creating an intervention committee of teachers, central-office staff, parents, and others—an all-hands-on-deck, "code red" response team—to address the problem before it leads to bigger issues, such as a spike in dropout rates.

Moreover, a high-reliability school district would have multiple ways to detect truancy rates; it wouldn't wait until May or June to learn that scores of students had been skipping class all year. These alarm bells could come in the form of classroom teachers reporting tardies and absences, schools collecting and reporting weekly data to the district, or community members and business owners reporting truants to school officials.

James Reason, a psychologist at the University of Manchester, England, who studies high-reliability systems, refers to this as the "Swiss cheese" model (Reason, 2000): Like Swiss cheese, any single layer has holes through which problems might slip. But when additional layers are added, it is increasingly unlikely that the holes within all the layers will align; a failure at one level will likely be caught at another level. Thus, high-reliability organizations depend on multiple layers to avert, monitor, and resolve failures in the system. In a school system, this might look very much like what the McKinsey report highlighted: hire the best teachers, help them be effective, and watch for indications that students need more help.

Every Defect a Treasure

High-reliability organizations encourage and reward error-reporting, even if those doing the reporting commit the errors themselves. In Japan, successful companies, most notably Toyota, adhere to the concept of *kaizen*—the continuous process of taking frequent and small steps on the path to improvement. A key principle of kaizen is that "every defect is a treasure." Making and uncovering mistakes are all part of the improvement process. A kaizen culture does not develop overnight and takes vigilance to maintain—a point illustrated by Toyota's recent woes in having to recall 8 million vehicles in response to reports that some cars have been accelerating uncontrollably. Auto industry analysts have observed that Toyota's problems arose because it lost sight of its core principle of kaizen and failed to rectify the problem swiftly before it mushroomed into a safety and public relations fiasco (Kelleher, 2010).

Karl Weick and Kathleen Sutcliffe provide an example of an organization that celebrates error-reporting in their 2001 book, *Managing the Unexpected: Assuring High Performance in an Age of Complexity.* Admiral Tom Mercer, former captain of the nuclear aircraft carrier *Carl Vinson*, tells the story of a sailor on board the ship who reported losing his wrench—a major concern on an aircraft carrier, as a wrench sucked into an aircraft engine could be catastrophic. All flight operations were halted until the wrench was found. Instead of being punished for his carelessness, the next day the sailor was commended in front of the crew.

A school-level corollary might be a culture where teachers are encouraged, and even rewarded, for reporting difficulties in helping students meet standards—for example, notifying the principal when what they are doing to help a student decode phonemes isn't working. As a result, the principal, like the ship admiral, could put "all hands on deck," providing the teacher and students with necessary supports and interventions to keep the students' reading difficulties from snowballing out of control.

In her book *It's Being Done: Academic Success in Unexpected Schools* (2007), Karin Chenoweth describes her visit to Oakland Heights Elementary School in Russellville, Arkansas. Despite having nearly three-quarters of its students qualify for free and reduced-price lunch, Oakland Heights is a rapidly improving school where black students pass the Arkansas state test at rates two to three times higher than students in the rest of the state. Upon arriving at the school, Chenoweth found lists, charts, and data sheets that tracked every student and every teacher. Data were the bedrock of how the school had made its dramatic improvements. For example, the school's principal, Sheri Shirley, knew from her constant monitoring of data that students in one classroom were mastering significantly more "sight" words (words read automatically without being sounded out) than students in other classrooms even though all teachers were using the same strategy: going through flash cards to help students master the words.

Left unchecked, of course, students' struggles with sight words could snowball into bigger problems. So Shirley observed teachers in all of the classrooms and discovered that in most classrooms, the teachers were simply reading the words to the children when they missed them. In the higher-performing classroom, the teacher would provide students with "tricks" to decode and remember the words—for example, identifying a "'word within a word' that the children already knew (st*AND*)" (Chenoweth, 2007, p. 44). By identifying the problem and "treasuring" the defect in kaizenlike fashion, Shirley was able to identify a simple, existing solution for improving students' acquisition of sight words. This twofold process of identifying error patterns as they occur and then quickly correcting them is at the heart of high-reliability organizations.

Creating a District "Dashboard"

Returning to the aviation metaphor that opened this chapter, what "gauges" should leaders monitor from the "flight deck" of the district office? What alarm bells and warning lights do they need? While a number of data points are important to monitor, it would seem that the two most necessary are dropout indicators and student academic performance.

Dropout indicators give districts a head start to avert the downward trajectory of a student failure. Research has identified several factors linked to a higher risk of dropping out, including lack of participation in extracurricular activities, frequent absenteeism, an unstable home environment, low family income, and having nongraduate parents (McNeil, Coppola, Radigan, & Heilig, 2008). As these predictors accumulate, so does a child's likelihood of dropping out of school. By collecting these data, school systems can pinpoint students who are likely candidates for additional support.

Certainly, districts already track and rely on student performance data. But not all data systems are created equal. The data from some systems are vague, easily misinterpreted, or slow in coming, which makes it impractical to use them to guide decision making.

One exemplary data-collection system is in place in the Minneapolis Public Schools. An oft-heard complaint about high-stakes assessment and accountability is that they may punish the "day shift" for shortcomings of the "night shift"—that is, teachers may struggle to get students to perform at grade level due to ineffective instruction provided the previous year. As a "value-added"

How to Avoid Drowning in Data

Schools and districts typically collect a stunning amount of data—some of it useful, some of it not. This can leave educators feeling as if they are adrift in a sea of data, with water, water everywhere, yet not a drop to drink. Here are a few simple ideas for making sense of it all.

Take an "onion approach" to analyzing achievement data. To zero in on real problems and avoid tilting at windmills, schools should approach their data as they would an onion, peeling back layers as they move from broad observations to more specific ones—for example, going from simply asking "How did students do on the state reading test?" to asking "Which questions did they struggle with?" and "Which students, in particular, struggled?"

Look for positive patterns as well as negative ones. Knowing what's going right is just as important as knowing what's going wrong. Success in one classroom, subject area, or group of students could surface strategies that could be replicated or highlight critical differences in approach that might be easily corrected.

Resist the urge to leap to conclusions. One of the biggest mistakes schools make is arriving at overly simplified explanations for what ails them. Low reading scores in 4th grade, for example, may have nothing to do with 4th grade at

Continued on next page ❯

How to Avoid Drowning in Data
(continued)

all—they could relate to a gap in the 2nd grade curriculum. That's why it's important to spend some time upfront simply making observations before asking *why* questions.

Ask why, again and again. A mistake schools often make is failing to address the root cause of their problems. When analyzing data, it's important to keep asking *why* until everyone is confident you've gotten to the heart of the problem. Why are a quarter of our 4th graders unable to identify parts of speech? Why did some learn it in 2nd grade and others didn't? Why did some teachers teach it and others didn't? Why haven't we included parts of speech in the curriculum guides?

Source: Adapted from *The Power of Data: Participant's Manual*, by D. Parsley, C. Dean, and J. Eck, 2005, Denver, CO: McREL.

assessment system, the Minneapolis model accounts for prior-year student performance to measure how much learning takes place during the school year (Ladd & Walsh, 2002). That way, a teacher who inherits a class testing on average at, say, the 20th percentile, is praised, not punished, for bringing students' scores up to the 40th percentile by the end of the school year.

Minneapolis's data system also statistically controls for free/reduced-price lunch status, English language learner status, special education status, gender, race, presence of a guardian in the child's home, and poverty level of the child's neighborhood. All of these factors provide a better estimate of the true contribution of a school to student performance. Thus, the district is able to identify and learn from schools that are changing the odds for their students.

From Theory to Results: The High Reliability Schools Project

Sam Stringfield's ideas on high-reliability schools were purely academic until David Reynolds, founding co-editor of the journal *School Effectiveness and School Improvement*, heard Stringfield present at a conference and later told a British audience about a "mad American" who had come up with the preposterous idea that schools could be operated with the same reliability as air traffic control towers (Stringfield et al., 2010). Afterward, a group of educators approached Reynolds and said, "Let's do it."

"Do what?" Reynolds asked.

Operate schools with the same reliability as air traffic control centers, they replied.

And so the High Reliability Schools project was born. From the outset, the project identified a set of general, research-based principles for teaching and schooling—the equivalent to standard operating procedures for classrooms and schools. It created professional development sessions around the principles, with the idea in mind that what was needed was not lockstep prescriptions for teaching but, rather, general principles that local educators (working in concert with college professors and other experts) could draw from to "co-construct" their own approaches to reform (Datnow & Stringfield, 2000).

One of the districts that signed on to the project was Neath-Port Talbot district in Wales. Once home to many thriving steel mills, the area had become a mere shadow of its former self, its factories closed and its population among the poorest in Wales. When the district signed on to the project, the 11 secondary schools in Neath-Port Talbot agreed to focus on two key goals. The first was to substantially increase the percentages of students passing five or more components of the British government's General Certificate of Secondary Education (GCSE) tests—a crucial, high-stakes test that often dictates students' future professions. The second was to improve attendance rates.

The reform effort itself focused on how to effectively—if not flawlessly—address many critical leverage points for improving student achievement, which, coincidentally, mirror the components of the What Matters Most framework identified in this book.

Ensuring High-Quality Instruction in Every Classroom

From the outset, to ensure consistent instruction in every classroom, the teachers of Neath-Port Talbot participated in extensive staff development that described research on effective teaching. The idea behind these sessions was to give teachers the information they needed to adapt some core principles of effective teaching to their own classrooms and students. To encourage consistent, high-quality instruction in every classroom, teachers engaged in peer observations through which they shared effective teaching techniques and offered one another critical feedback when needed.

Providing Challenging Curricular Pathways

One of the district's initial concerns was that some primary schools were unintentionally setting low expectations for student achievement. To help them understand expectations for students at the secondary level, leaders from the low-performing primary schools attended staff development with their counterparts at secondary schools. One secondary school even went so far as to use its own funds to support a literacy coordinator in its four feeder schools to help align curriculum and teaching expectations.

Providing a Robust System of Student Supports

To improve their system of student supports, the district created SOPs for identifying students at risk of failure and providing them with intensive, schoolwide interventions. Teachers gave every student short tests at the beginning of the year and then met as grade-level teams to discuss how to address students' individual learning needs.

Creating High-Performance School Cultures

Stringfield and the others guiding the reform initiative understood from the outset that what school leaders were asking their teachers to do was effect monumental change in school culture. For example, they were asking teachers to go from isolated classrooms, where they could pretty much do what they wanted, to a far more collaborative culture, where teachers were expected to work together, share practices, and, when necessary, give one another critical feedback. Thus, a core component of the entire effort was to provide school leaders with professional development in managing change. In addition, to foster a districtwide culture of high performance, school leaders were asked to share with one another how they were raising the bar for curriculum and instruction during sessions that came to be called "the little things that matter" (p. 19).

Using Data Systems to Create a High-Reliability Organization

At the heart of the entire effort in Neath-Port Talbot was the creation of a sophisticated data system that tracked student achievement data, provided value-added calculations for schools and teachers, and stored relevant background information on students. Teachers and school leaders received extensive training on how to use this system to identify, in real time, students in need of additional learning supports. For example, when it was discovered that many 11-year-olds were entering secondary school more than two years behind in reading, alarm bells went off in the district office, which responded by launching an immediate, large-scale effort to coordinate literacy programs across both primary and secondary schools.

Results: One School's Story

One secondary school that signed on to the project was Sandfield, a particularly disadvantaged secondary school located within a government housing project. Prior to the start of the initiative, its percentage of students passing the GCSE tests had sunk so low that the government was threatening to close it. Knowing that it needed a "quick win" to energize and transform its culture, the school launched an effort to clean up its grounds and facilities, which had fallen into considerable disrepair. With the help of the surrounding community, the quite literal "Broken Windows" campaign gave the entire school a much-needed facelift. Within a matter of weeks, the school's appearance improved dramatically, giving the students and faculty a new sense of hope and optimism that things were finally turning around for the school.

Over the new few years, student achievement rose steadily at the school. In its darkest days, getting a quarter of its students to pass five GCSE tests would have been ambitious. Within a few years, though, more than half of its students were passing the tests—a feat that would have seemed unimaginable a few years before.

The Touchstones

For some readers, the key observations made to this point in this book may seem, well, a bit ordinary. Providing students with good instruction, challenging curricula, supports when they fall behind, and a school environment that encourages them to succeed are not exactly new ideas. Recall, though, that while they may not be earthshaking, they are the "high-payoff" leverage points that can dramatically change the odds for student success.

So, yes, while they may not be the new flavor of the month, these "plain vanilla" factors *are* what matters most for student success. And let's be clear. While the individual components of the What Matters Most framework may not be new, putting them all together in a consistent way with near flawless execution, across an entire system, *would* be new.

This idea—doing well what we already know needs to be done—is the essence of high-reliability systems. While much has been written about high-reliability organizations in general, education research suggests that school systems would do well to attend to the following touchstones for functioning as high-reliability organizations.

Setting clear, "no excuses" goals for teaching and learning. Just as an airline or nuclear power plant would never set a goal of being anything less than disaster free, school systems should focus on ensuring the success of 100 percent of its children. While 100 percent proficiency is certainly the aim of the No Child Left Behind Act, these goals have probably not been internalized by everyone in the system. Research suggests that high-performing systems take the time to set goals collaboratively to ensure buy-in among stakeholder groups. Moreover, simply setting a goal does not mean it will get accomplished; high-performing systems also identify clear strategies they will take to reach their goals.

Attending to the "core" business of schooling: consistently high-quality instruction. Because teaching and learning are the "core business" of school systems, they must focus on filling every classroom, in every school, with a great teacher.

Developing a healthy, data-driven preoccupation with failure, prevention, and intervention. Failures occur in even the best systems. To ensure high reliability, school systems must adopt data and diagnostic systems that identify error patterns as soon as they occur, putting in place processes for responding to them and learning from failures in the spirit of kaizen, or continuous improvement.

To date, most of the literature on high-reliability organizations focuses on such systems as nuclear plants, chemical processing facilities, aircraft carriers, and air traffic control towers—all systems guided (out of necessity) by standardized procedures and regulations. For some, the image of these systems may be of people following rigid, mechanistic tasks (for example, pilots methodically working through a lengthy preflight checklist)—a far cry from what educators experience in the complex, ever-changing environment of schools and classrooms, where each day brings a new challenge or the wonderful opportunity of an unanticipated teachable moment.

High-reliability organizations, however, are not dreary places where people mindlessly follow procedures with no ability to think creatively or innovatively. To the contrary, they are mindful organizations. Hoy, Gage, and Tarter (2006) identified several distinguishing characteristics of high-performing schools. Among them is "deference to expertise, not authority." That is, people at all levels of the system are developed as experts who are encouraged to ask questions, raise issues, and make on-the-spot decisions.

Creating High-Reliability District Systems: A Sample Checklist

Setting clear, "no excuses" goals for teaching and learning

☐ Districtwide goals for teaching and learning are identified and articulated

☐ District resources are aligned with goals

☐ A consistent, districtwide approach to instruction is articulated

Attending to the "core" business of schooling: great teachers and teaching

☐ Processes to recruit and retain the best teachers possible are in place

☐ Staff development is coordinated to support individual teachers' growth

☐ Fair, consistent teacher evaluations are conducted that improve performance

Developing a healthy, data-driven preoccupation with failure, prevention, and intervention

☐ Data systems that track student achievement and dropout indicators are present

☐ Standard operating procedures for responding to student failure are followed

6

Living by the Book, but Not Dying by It

On September 26, 1983, Stanislav Petrov, a 44-year-old lieutenant colonel in the Russian army, sat in his commander's chair in a secret bunker south of Moscow. His job: to monitor data from Soviet satellites trained on the airspace between the United States and the Soviet Union.

Shortly after midnight, a red button in front of Petrov began to flash: a U.S. nuclear missile was on its way to the Soviet Union. Petrov was a critical link in the Soviet chain of command, supervising the team that monitored incoming messages from Soviet intelligence satellites. Upon first warning of a U.S. attack, he had been instructed to act fast: The missile would enter Russian airspace within minutes. To give the Soviets ample time for a counterattack, he was to report any such incident immediately to superiors.

Suddenly, a second missile appeared, then another, and another. Soon, the warning system was "roaring." Five U.S. missiles were apparently on their way, bringing nuclear annihilation to their Soviet targets.

The easy thing for Petrov to have done, of course, would have been to simply follow orders, pick up the phone, and report the attack to his superiors. Under tremendous stress, Petrov agonized over what to do. If he reported the missiles, the Soviet high command would most likely order a global counter-attack, quite possibly bringing about the end of human civilization. Yet, as he later recalled, he found himself thinking, "When people start a war, they don't start it with only five missiles. You can do little damage with just five missiles" (Hoffman, 1999, A19).

Finally, he decided to ignore the flashing screens in front of him. "I had a funny feeling in my gut," Petrov later told a *Washington Post* reporter. "I didn't want to make a mistake. I made a decision, and that was it" (A19).

Petrov's instincts were right. The United States had not launched an attack; the Soviet satellite system had mistaken the sun's reflection off clouds for missiles.

Petrov's actions exemplify a key trait of members of high-reliability organizations (HROs): They are willing to live by the book but not *die* by it. While Petrov knew the rules and regulations of his job, he also knew its true purpose: to keep Russia safe from attack. Raising a false alarm and bringing about an all-out nuclear war would have been contrary to that purpose. (*Note:* in a true HRO, Petrov would have been rewarded for his actions. Instead, he was grilled by superiors, who tried to make him a scapegoat for the incident. In the end, he was neither punished nor rewarded, because doing so would have made his superiors look bad and called attention to flaws in the warning system.)

The Banality of Bad Decisions

Contrast Petrov's story with a recent incident in Forest Hills, New York. Alexa Gonzalez, a 12-year-old junior high student, wrote on her desk with a green marker: "I love my friends Abby and Faith. Lex was here 2/1/10 :)." Alexa's first mistake, of course, was writing on her desk; her second was signing her name to her handiwork. When school officials discovered the defaced property, she expected a lecture or maybe detention; this was, after all, her first offense. Instead, her principal phoned the police, who came to school, handcuffed Alexa, and led her across the street to the police precinct (Chen, 2010).

Her principal was just following the rules: New York's "zero tolerance" policies for school safety. Alexa's suspension from school was eventually rescinded, but the incident paints a dismaying picture of a school system where well-meaning adults feel compelled to make irrational decisions that have detrimental effects on students—to die by the book. Why not simply make Alexa stay after school to clean the desk and, for good measure, every other desk in the classroom?

Alexa's principal is not a bad or small-minded person. To the contrary, the principal's actions probably reflect a rational response to an irrational system, one where educators feel so hide-bound by rules, regulations, and countless programs and initiatives that they can lose sight of what matters most. As a result, they engage in behaviors that seem void of common sense.

Breaking Rules, Following Principles

In the late 1970s and early 1980s, Sy Fliegel, a deputy superintendent in charge of alternative schools in New York City, faced a dilemma. One of the city's schools, Central Park East, a combined elementary and secondary school, was demonstrating dramatic results for its low-income students: 85 percent of its high school students were receiving full diplomas and another 11 percent GEDs—almost double the citywide averages.

The school's leader, Deborah Meier, who insisted on calling herself a "teacher-leader," had pulled together a team of inspired teachers into a "staff-run" school (Meier, 1995, p. 25). The magic of the school, Fliegel understood, was its teachers, who were remarkable, in Meier's words, not because "they went to more elite colleges, [had] taught longer, or [had] exceptional gifts" but because "they were practic[ing] what they believed in"—namely, a new way of student-centered teaching that they had helped to design (p. 37).

The dilemma for Fliegel lay in the district's staffing rules. The rules said that veteran teachers, those with something called "building tenure," got first dibs on job openings anywhere in the district. Both Fliegel and Meier worried that if Central Park East posted its job openings publicly, the school would be forced to hire a "cadre of burned-out teachers," the infusion of which would likely ruin the very thing that made the school function so well: its culture and unique teacher camaraderie (p. 34). In other words, following district staffing rules would likely destroy the magic of Central Park East.

Fliegel could have decided, of course, that "rules are rules" and simply followed them. It would have been an easy decision to make—as easy as phoning superiors about blips on a radar screen or calling the police when a student defaced a desk.

Instead, he decided to engage in an act of what he called "creative noncompliance" (Meier, 2007). He bent (some might say broke) several staff rules, including hiding the openings at Central Park East from the rest of the district, thus giving Meier time to surreptitiously recruit teachers she believed would maintain its culture (Mathews, 2010). In short, Fliegel didn't let arbitrary staffing *rules* get in the way of the more important *principles* of guaranteeing high-quality, challenging instruction and creating a school culture of high expectations.

Get Creative

A key point to make here is that the touchstones identified in this book are not rules but *principles*. As screenwriting guru Robert McKee, whose disciples have won 32 Academy Awards for screenplays, has noted, rules are different than principles.

> A rule says, "You must do it this way." A principle says, "This works ... and has through all remembered time." The difference is crucial. Your work needn't be modeled after the "well-made" play; rather, it must be well made within the principles that shape our art. Anxious, inexperienced writers obey rules. Rebellious, unschooled writers break rules. Artists master the form [the principles]. (McKee, 1997, p. 18)

These same ideas apply to educators. In mindful organizations, people follow principles, not rules. Like Stanislav Petrov or Sy Fliegel, they know the rules of their jobs. Petrov understood that when missiles appeared on his radar screen, he was *supposed* to pick up the phone and call his superiors. Fliegel knew that when vacancies opened up in schools, he was *supposed* to let teachers with seniority, regardless of their quality, learn about and get those jobs. Fortunately, both men comprehended the guiding principles of their jobs—the *why* behind the *what*. As a result, they understood what to do when the rules of their jobs conflicted with their purpose.

How-to guidance without clarity of purpose can lead to mindless, automaton-like behavior. Thus, my focus in this book has been to help educators return to the touchstones—the *whys* of what they're doing. As McKee tells screenwriters, following principles need not make anyone less creative or innovative. Indeed, I hope that those who have read this book will be more mindful of the simple, key principles of school systems so that they, too, can become master artisans who focus their creativity and ingenuity on doing what matters most to change the odds for all students.

Final Thoughts: The Other Side of Complexity

It's been said that there are two types of people in this world: those who divide the world into two types of people and those who don't. In short, there are simplifiers and complexifiers.

Most people probably fancy themselves as simplifiers—no-nonsense, "cut to the chase" kind of people who roll their eyes at elaborate flow charts and diagrams and just want to get down to the brass tacks of what's important.

In reality, though, nuance, "yeah, buts," and conflicting data often get in the way of our simplicity. Soon, we find ourselves creating bulleted lists three indentations deep to explain what, when we set out, seemed like a simple matter. Then we find ourselves standing up in meetings and declaring, "If we just remember to do these 47 things, people, we should be OK." We're met with eye rolling and people wondering privately, if not publicly, Can't you simplify this?

As I noted in the Introduction, the purpose of this book has been to work through the complexity and cacophony of hundreds of research reports, anecdotes, and concepts, to identify a few, simple principles at the heart of what it will take to help all students become successful learners. The result of this distillation is the five components and associated touchstones of the What Matters Most framework (see Figure 6.1).

Given the many sidebars, anecdotes, touchstones, and checklists sprinkled throughout this book, I myself might be accused of needlessly complexifying these five components. In the event that they've decreased the "signal-to-noise" ratio and inadvertently broken up the message at the heart of this book, let me return to it now.

At the heart of all of these components and touchstones are actually just *two* very simple ideas for what it will take to change the odds for students. We see these two, somewhat paradoxical concepts at play in research on effective practices throughout the system—in what makes a good teacher, curriculum, school environment, and district system. Indeed, as you've been reading, you may have found these themes popping up over and over again, recurring throughout this book.

Figure 6.1
The What Matters Most Framework Components and Their Touchstones

What Matters Most	Touchstones
Guaranteeing challenging, engaging, and intentional instruction	*Teachers must focus on* • Setting high expectations and delivering challenging instruction. • Fostering engaging learning environments and meaningful relationships with students. • Intentionally matching instructional strategies to learning goals.
Ensuring curricular pathways to success	*School systems must focus on* • Providing all students with high-expectations curricula. • Providing all students with personalized learning opportunities.
Providing whole-child student supports	*School systems must focus on* • Providing real-time supports in keeping with the ounce-of-prevention principle. • Addressing the deep causes of student performance: home environment, prior knowledge, interest, and motivation.
Creating high-performance school cultures	*School leaders must focus on* • Raising the quality and reducing the variability among classrooms within the school. • Creating a school culture of high expectations for academics and behavior.
Developing data-driven, high-reliability district systems	*School systems must focus on* • Setting clear, "no excuses" goals for teaching and learning. • Attending to the core business of schooling: great teachers and teaching. • Developing a healthy preoccupation with failure, prevention, and intervention.

Here they are, the two deep principles—the yin and yang, if you will, at the heart of all five components and their touchstones: *challenge* and *support*:

- Teachers must *challenge* students with high expectations and *support* them by developing meaningful relationships and providing instruction that addresses their learning needs.

- Curriculum must *challenge* students with high expectations while *supporting* their intrinsic motivation to learn with personalized learning opportunities.

- Schools must *challenge* students with high expectations for behavior and learning while providing them with whole-child *support*.

- School leaders must *challenge* teachers to improve performance and *support* their professional growth.

- The system must *challenge* everyone in it by setting high goals for schools, teachers, and learners while providing a data-driven system of *support* for struggling schools, teachers, and students.

This balance of high expectations with strong supports is not a new idea: it's reflected in Judith Kleinfeld's (1972) concept of teachers as "warm demanders," who balance expectations with nurturing. It's also evident in Charles Payne's "authoritative-supportive" model of teaching, which combines high levels of intellectual demand with "holistic concern" for students, or what some call the "new paternalism" in effective schools—schools that provide "prescriptive yet warm" learning environments where teachers are "both authoritative and caring figures" (Payne, 2008, p. 22; Whitman, 2008, p. 54).

To be certain, nothing about these simple principles is *easy*—indeed, nothing worth doing ever is. If, however, we as educators can thoughtfully, effectively, and consistently apply these two principles in every aspect of the system, the preponderance of research suggests that we can have a tremendous impact on student success.

Nearly everyone who gets into education does so because he or she wants to make a difference in the lives of students. The hopeful message of this book is that we *can* make a tremendous difference for students—especially if everyone is on the same page and working to the same ends. We don't need to wait for "Superman" or some new innovation to improve students' lives. We can start tomorrow by simply doing better what decades of research says matters most to change the odds for student success.

The What Matters Most System Survey

See how well your school or district is addressing the *Simply Better* "touchstones" at http://survey.changetheodds.org. Take the free, 20-minute quiz to identify your school or district's strengths as well as areas where focused improvements are likely to change the odds for student success.

References

ACT, Inc. (2008). *2008 ACT national profile report*. Iowa City, IA: Author.

American Council on Education. (2008). *Minorities in higher education 2008 twenty-third status report*. Washington, DC: Author.

Baker, S., Gersten, R., & Lee, D. S. (2002). A synthesis of empirical research on teaching mathematics to low-achieving students. *Elementary School Journal, 10*, 51–73.

Barrett, C. (2008, May). Colleen's corner: Talking Southwest culture. *Southwest Airlines Spirit Magazine* 12.

Baum, S., & Payea, K. (2004). *Education pays 2004: The benefits of higher education for individuals and society*. New York: The College Board.

Bellamy, G. T., Crawford, L., Marshall, L. H., & Coulter, G. A. (2005). The fail-safe schools challenge: Leadership possibilities from high reliability organizations. *Educational Administration Quarterly, 41*(3), 383–412.

Blair, C., & Razza, R. P. (2007). Relating effortful control, executive function, and false belief understanding to emerging math and literacy ability in kindergarten. *Child Development, 78*(2), 647–663.

Bloom, H., Thompson, S. L., & Unterman, R., with Herlihy, C., & Payne, C. F. (2010). *Transforming the high school learning experience: How New York City's small schools are boosting achievement and graduation rates*. New York: MDRC.

Bodrova, E., Leong, D., Paynter, D., & Hensen, R. (2001). *Scaffolding literacy development in the preschool classroom*. Aurora, CO: McREL.

Bodrova, E., Leong, D. J., Paynter, D. E., & Hensen, R. (2003). *Scaffolding literacy development in the preschool classroom* (rev. ed.). Aurora, CO: McREL.

Bradby, D., Malloy, A., Hanna, T., & Dayton, C. (2007, March). *A profile of the California Partnership Academies, 2004–2005.* Berkeley: California Center for College and Career.

Braun, E. (n.d.). Are we ready to reinvent our management? *HSM Global.* Retrieved from http://us.hsmglobal.com/notas/57129-are-we-ready-to-reinvent-our-management

Brickhouse, T. C., & Smith, N. D. (2000). *The philosophy of Socrates.* Boulder, CO: Westview Press.

Bridgeland, J. M., Dilulio, J., & Morison, K. B. (2006). *The silent epidemic: Perspectives of high school dropouts.* Washington, DC: Civic Enterprises.

Bronson, P., & Merryman, A. (2009). *NurtureShock.* New York: Hatchette Book Group.

Bryk, A. S., Sebring, P. B., Kerbow, D., Rollow, S., & Easton, J. Q. (1998). *Charting Chicago school reform: Democratic localism as a lever for change.* Boulder, CO: Westview Press.

Carpenter, W. A. (2000). Ten years of silver bullets: Dissenting thoughts on education reform. *Phi Delta Kappan, (81)*5, 383.

Centers, J. (2008, August 26). Superintendent Charlotte Ciancio may have super powers. *Westword.* Retrieved from http://www.westword.com/2008-08-28/news/superintendent-charlotte-ciancio-may-have-super-powers

Changing the Odds for Students at Risk. (2008, December 1). Panel discussion, New American Foundation, Washington, D.C. Retrieved from http://www.newamerica.net/events/2008/changing_odds

Chen, S. (2010). Girl's arrest for doodling raises concerns about zero tolerance. *CNN.* Retrieved from http://www.cnn.com/2010/CRIME/02/18/new.york.doodle.arrest.index.html?iref=allsearch

Chenoweth, K. (2007). *It's being done: Academic success in unexpected schools.* Cambridge, MA: Harvard Education Press.

Chenoweth, K. (2009). *How It's being done: Urgent lessons from unexpected schools.* Cambridge, MA: Harvard Education Press.

Cialdini, R. B. (2005). What's the best secret device for engaging student interest? Hint: The answer's in the title. *Journal of Social and Clinical Psychology, 24*(1), 22–29.

College Board. (2009). *Annual AP program participation 1956–2009.* Retrieved from http://professionals.collegeboard.com/profdownload/annual-participation-09.pdf

College Board. (2010). *6th annual AP report to the nation* [additional data]. Retrieved from http://www.collegeboard.com/html/aprtn/theme_1_wider_segment .html?expandable=0

Collins, J. (2001). *Good to great: Why some companies make the leap and others don't.* New York: HarperCollins.

Comer, J. P., Haynes, N. M., & Joyner, J. T. (1996). The school development program. In J. P. Comer, N. M. Haynes, J. T. Joyner, & M. Ben-Avie (Eds.), *Rallying the whole village: The Comer process for reforming education.* New York: Teachers College Press.

Commission to Build a Healthier America. (2009, September). *Education and health: Education matters for health* (Issue Brief 6). Washington, DC: Robert Wood Johnson Foundation.

Conley, D. T. (2007). *Toward a more comprehensive conception of college readiness.* Eugene, OR: Educational Policy Improvement Center.

Cooper, H. (1994). Homework research and policy: A review of the literature. *Research/Practice, 2*(2). Retrieved from http://www.cehd.umn.edu/carei/reports/ Rpractice/Summer94/homework.html

Cornelius-White, J. (2007). Learner-centered teacher–student relationships are effective: A meta-analysis. *Review of Educational Research, 77*(1), 113–143.

Datnow, A., & Stringfield, S. (2000). Working together for reliable school reform. *Journal of Education for Students Placed at Risk, 5*(1&2), 183–204.

Delorenzo, R. A., Battino, W. J., Schreiber, R. M., & Gaddy Carrio, B. B. (2009). *Delivering on the promise: The education revolution.* Bloomington, IN: Solution Tree Press.

Duncan, G. J., & Magnuson, K. A. (2005). Can family socioeconomic resources account for racial and ethnic test score gaps? *The Future of Children, 15*(1), 35–54.

Dweck, C. (2006). *Mindset.* New York: Random House.

Fan, X., & Chen, M. (1999, April 19–23). Parental involvement and students' academic achievement. Paper presented at the annual meeting of the American Educational Research Association, Montreal, Quebec.

Farkas, S., Johnson, J., & Duffet, A. (2003). *Stand by me: What teachers really think about unions, merit pay and other professional matters.* New York: Public Agenda.

Felch, J., Song, J., & Smith, J. (2010, August 14). Who's teaching L.A.'s kids? A *Times* analysis, using data largely ignored by LAUSD, looks at which educators help students learn, and which hold them back. *Los Angeles Times.* Retrieved from http://www.latimes.com/news/local/la-me-teachers-value- 20100815,0,6178994,print.story

Flaherty, L. T., & Weist, M. D. (1999). School-based mental health services: The Baltimore models. *Psychology in the Schools, 36*(5), 379–389.

Flowers, T. A., & Flowers, L. A. (2008). Factors affecting urban African American high school students' achievement in reading. *Urban Education, 43*(2), 154–172.

Galvin, M. (2007, Spring). "Fractal" experiences, quick wins, and school successes. *Changing Schools, 55,* 1–12.

Galvin, M., & Parsley, D. (2005). Turning failure into opportunity. *Educational Leadership, 62* [online only]. Retrieved from http://www.ascd.org/publications/educational-leadership/summer05/vol62/num09/Turning-Failure-Into-Opportunity.aspx

Gardner, H. (2006). *Multiple intelligences.* New York: Basic Books.

Gawande, A. (2007). *Better: A surgeon's notes on performance.* New York: Picador.

Gawande, A. (2009). *The checklist manifesto: How to get things right.* New York: Metropolitan Books.

Geiser, P. (2009, December 20). Promoting grade inflation. *The New York Times.* Retrieved from http://roomfordebate.blogs.nytimes.com/2009/12/20/the-advanced-placement-juggernaut

Geiser, S., & Santelices, V. (2004). *The role of Advanced Placement and honors courses in college admissions.* Berkeley: University of California, Center for Studies in Higher Education. Retrieved from http://cshe.berkeley.edu/publications/papers/papers.html

Gentner, D., Loewenstein, J., Thompson, L., & Forbus, K. D. (2009). Reviving inert knowledge: Analogical abstraction supports relational retrieval of past events. *Cognitive Science, 33,* 1343–1382.

Gladwell, M. (2000). *The tipping point: How little things can make a big difference.* New York: Little, Brown and Company.

Gladwell, M. (2005). *Blink: The Power of Thinking Without Thinking,* New York: Little, Brown and Company.

Goldberg, M. F. (1990). Portrait of Dennis Littky. *Educational Leadership, 47*(8), 28.

Gonzalez, L. (2009). *Everyday survival: Why smart people do stupid things.* New York: W. W. Norton & Company.

Gorey, K. M. (2001). Early childhood education: A meta-analytic affirmation of the short- and long-term benefits of educational opportunity. *School Psychology Quarterly, 16*(1), 9–30.

Greene, J., & Foster, G. (2003). *Public high school graduation and college readiness rates in the United States.* New York: Center for Civic Information at the Manhattan Institute.

Guggenheim, D. (Director). (2010). *Waiting for "Superman"* [Motion picture]. United States: Paramount.

Hall, T. (2002). *Differentiated instruction.* Wakefield, MA: National Center on Accessing the General Curriculum. Retrieved from http://www.cast.org/publications/ncac/ncac_diffinstruc.html

Hanson, R. R. (2008). *Early interventions for the achievement gap: The importance of family in early learning.* Washington, DC: National Urban League Policy Institute.

Hanushek, E. (1998). *The evidence on class size.* Rochester, NY: W. Allen Wallis Institute of Political Economy, University of Rochester.

Hanushek, E. A. (2002). Teacher quality. In L. T. Izumi & W. M. Evers (Eds.), *Teacher quality.* Stanford, CA: Hoover Press. Retrieved from http://edpro.stanford.edu/hanushek/admin/pages/files/uploads/Teacher%20quality.Evers-Izumi.pdf

Harlow, C. W. (2003). *Education and correctional populations.* Washington, DC: U.S. Department of Justice, Bureau of Justice Statistics.

Hart, B., & Risley, R. (1995). *Meaningful differences in the everyday experience of young American children.* Baltimore, MD: Paul H. Brookes Publishing.

Hattie, J. (2009). *Visible learning: A synthesis of over 800 meta-analyses relating to achievement.* New York: Routledge.

Heath, C., & Heath, D. (2007). *Made to stick: Why some ideas survive and others die.* New York: Random House.

Hensch, T. K. (2005). Critical period mechanisms in developing visual cortex. *Current Topics in Developmental Biology, 69*, 215–237.

Hodgkinson, H. L. (2003). *Leaving too many children behind: A demographer's view on the neglect of America's youngest children.* Washington, DC: Institute for Educational Leadership. (ERIC Document Reproduction Service No. ED 476 949).

Hoffman, D. (1999, February 10). Shattered shield: "I had a funny feeling in my gut." *Washington Post*, A19.

Hofstadter, D. (1979). *Gödel, Escher, Bach: An eternal golden braid.* New York: Basic Books.

Hollingsworth, J., & Ybarra, S. (2009). *Explicit direct instruction (EDI): The power of the well-crafted, well-taught lesson.* Thousand Oaks, CA: Corwin.

Howell, E., & McFeeters, J. (2008). Children's mental health care: Differences by race/ethnicity in urban/rural areas. *Journal of Health Care for the Poor and Underserved, 19*(1), 237–247.

Hoy, W. K., Gage, Q., & Tarter, C. J. (2006). School mindfulness and faculty trust: Necessary conditions for each other. *Educational Administration Quarterly, 42*, 236–255.

Hoy, W. K., Tarter, C. J., & Hoy, A. W. (2006). Academic optimism of schools: A force for student achievement. *American Educational Research Journal, 43*(3), 440.

James-Burdumy, S., Dynarski, M., Moore, M., Deke, J., Mansfield, W., & Pistorino, C. (2005). *When schools stay open late: The national evaluation of the 21st Century Community Learning Centers program: Final report.* U.S. Department of Education, Institute of Education Sciences, National Center for Education Evaluation and Regional Assistance. Retrieved from http://www.ed.gov/ies/ncee

Johnson, R. T., & Johnson, D. W. (n.d.). Encouraging student/student interaction. In *Research matters—to the science teacher.* Reston, VA: National Association for Research in Science Teaching. Retrieved from http://www.narst.org/publications/research/encourage2.cfm

Juszczak, L., Melinkovich, P., & Kaplan, D. (2003). Use of health and mental health services by adolescents across multiple delivery sites. *Journal of Adolescent Health, 32*(6, suppl.), 108–118.

Kammeraad-Campbell, S. (1990). *Doc: The story of Dennis Littky and his fight for a better school.* New York: Contemporary Books.

Kavale, K. A., & Forness, S. R. (1987). Substance over style: Assessing the efficacy of modality testing and teaching. *Exceptional Children, 54*(3), 228–239.

Kelleher, J. B. (2010, February 8). Toyota stumbles but its "kaizen" cult endures. *Reuters.* Retrieved from http://www.reuters.com/article/idUSTRE6161RV20100208

Kemple, J. J., with Willner, C. J. (2008). *Career academies: Long-term impacts on labor market outcomes, educational attainment, and transitions to adulthood.* New York: MDRC.

Kingon, J. (2001, April 8). A view from the trenches. *The New York Times.* Retrieved from http://www.nytimes.com/2001/04/08/education/08ED-KING.html?pagewanted=print

Kirschner, P. A., Sweller, J., & Clark, R. E. (2006). Why minimal guidance during instruction does not work: An analysis of the failure of constructivist, discovery, problem-based, experiential, and inquiry-based teaching. *Educational Psychologist, 41*(2), 75–86.

Klein, J., Rhee, M., et al. (2010, October 10). How to fix our schools: A manifesto from Joel Klein, Michelle Rhee and others. *Washington Post,* B1. Retrieved from http://www.washingtonpost.com/wp-dyn/content/article/2010/10/07/AR2010100705078_pf.html

Kleinfeld, J. (1972). *Effective teachers of Indian and Eskimo high school students.* Fairbanks: University of Alaska, Institute of Social, Economic, and Government Research.

Kleinfeld, J. (1975). Effective teachers of Eskimo and Indian students. *School Review, 83,* 301–304.

Kleinfeld, J. (1994). Learning styles and culture. In W. Lonner & R. Malpass (Eds.), *Psychology and culture* (pp. 151–156). Boston: Allyn & Bacon.

Konstantopoulos, S. (2005). *Trends of school effects on student achievement: Evidence from NLS:72, HSB:82, and NELS:92.* Bonn, Germany: Institute for the Study of Labor.

Ladd, H. F., & Walsh, R. P. (2002). Implementing value-added measures of school effectiveness: Getting the incentives right. *Economics of Education Review, 21*(1), 1–17.

Lauer, P. A., Akiba, M., Wilkerson, S. B., Apthorp, H. S., Snow, D., & Martin-Glenn, M. (2004). *The effectiveness of out-of-school-time strategies in assisting low-achieving students in reading and mathematics: A research synthesis* (rev. ed.). Aurora, CO: McREL.

Lemov, D. (2010). *Teach like a champion: 49 techniques that put students on the path to college.* San Francisco: Jossey-Bass.

Levin, J., & Quinn, M. (2003). *Missed opportunities: How we keep high-quality teachers out of urban schools.* New York: The New Teacher Project.

Lewis, M. (2006). *The blind side: Evolution of a game.* New York: W. W. Norton & Company.

Littky, D. (2010). Dennis Littky's view: Time goes by, everything looks the same. *Interactions.* Retrieved September 13, 2010, from http://www.bigpicture .org/2010/07/time-goes-by-everything-looks-the-same/

Littky, D., & Grabelle, S. (2004). *The big picture: Education is everyone's business.* Alexandria, VA: ASCD.

Marzano, R. J. (2000). *A new era of school reform: Going where the research takes us.* Aurora, CO: McREL.

Marzano, R. J. (2003). *What works in schools: Translating research into action.* Alexandria, VA: ASCD.

Marzano, R. J., Marzano, J. S., & Pickering, D. (2003). *Classroom management that works: Research-based strategies for every teacher.* Alexandria, VA: ASCD.

Marzano, R. J., & Pickering, D. J., with Arredondo, D. E., Blackburn, G. J., Brandt, R. S., Moffett, C. A., Paynter, D. E., Pollock, J. E., & Whisler, J. (1997). *Dimensions of learning: Teacher's manual* (2nd ed.). Alexandria, VA: ASCD.

Marzano, R. J., Pickering, D. J., & Pollock, J. E. (2001). *Classroom instruction that works: Research-based strategies for increasing student achievement.* Alexandria, VA: ASCD.

Marzano, R., & Waters, T. (2009). *District leadership that works: Striking the right balance.* Bloomington, IN: Solution Tree.

Marzano, R. J., Waters, T., & McNulty, B. A. (2005). *School leadership that works: From research to results.* Alexandria, VA: ASCD.

Massey, R. (2007, November 7). British Airways flight seconds away from mid-air disaster. *Daily Mail.* Retrieved from http://www.dailymail.co.uk/news/article-492128/British-Airways-flight-seconds-away-mid-air-disaster.html

Mathews, J. (1988). *Escalante: The best teacher in America.* New York: Henry Holt & Company.

Mathews, J. (2007, May 28). Education: Why they are the best. *Washington Post.* Retrieved from http://www.newsweek.com/id/34478

Mathews, J. (2008a, May 14). A Challenge Index boycott of sorts. *Washington Post.* Retrieved from http://www.washingtonpost.com/wp-dyn/content/article/2008/04/14/AR2008041400545_pf.html

Mathews, J. (2008b, December 11). Why I changed the Challenge Index. *Washington Post.* Retrieved from http://www.washingtonpost.com/wp-dyn/content/article/2008/12/11/AR2008121100744_pf.html

Mathews, J. (2009). *Work hard, be nice: How two inspired teachers created the most promising schools in America.* Chapel Hill, NC: Algonquin Books of Chapel Hill.

Mathews, J. (2010, July 12). Results of D.C. principal's controversial methods need to outweigh criticism. *Washington Post,* B2. Retrieved from http://www.washingtonpost.com/wp-dyn/content/article/2010/07/11/AR2010071103470_pf.html

McCartney, S. (2010, January 28). The money ledger: Tallying 2009 airline profits and losses. *Wall Street Journal.* Retrieved from http://blogs.wsj.com/middleseat/2010/01/28/which-airlines-made-lost-money-last-year/

McKee, R. (1997). *Story: Substance, structure, style and the principles of screenwriting.* New York: Harper Collins.

McKinsey & Company. (2007). *How the world's best-performing school systems come out on top.* Retrieved from http://www.mckinsey.com/App_Media/Reports/SSO/Worlds_School_Systems_Final.pdf

McNeil, L. M., Coppola, E., Radigan, J., & Heilig, J. V. (2008). Avoidable losses: High-stakes accountability and the dropout crisis. *Education Policy Analysis Archives, 16*(3), 1–48.

McREL. (n.d.). Alcester-Hudson Elementary School, Alcester, South Dakota [webpage]. Retrieved March 3, 2011, from http://www.mcrel.org/success-in-sight/alcester-hudson-south-dakota.asp

McREL. (2005a). *McREL insights: Professional development analysis.* Aurora, CO: Author.

McREL. (2005b). *McREL insights: Schools that "beat the odds."* Aurora, CO: Author.

Medina, J. (2008). *Brain rules: 12 principles for surviving and thriving at work, home, and school.* Seattle, WA: Pear Press.

Meier, D. (1995). *The power of their ideas: Lessons for America from a small school in Harlem.* Boston: Beacon Press.

Meier, D. (2007, September 13). Bringing honest exchange into kids' lives [blog entry]. *Education Week.* Retrieved from http://blogs.edweek.org/edweek/Bridging-Differences/2007/09/bringing_honest_exchange_into.html

Meyer, J. (2010, August 17). Colorado school districts a study in reform. *Denver Post.* Retrieved from http://www.denverpost.com/news/ci_15800152

Mitchell, N. (2009, July 21). Numbers show teacher evaluation system broken. *Education News Colorado.* Retrieved January 9, 2010. from http://www.ednewscolorado.org/2009/07/21/numbers-show-teacher-evaluation-system-broken/

Nasir, S. N., Hand, V., & Taylor, E. V. (2008). Culture and mathematics in school: Boundaries between "cultural" and "domain" knowledge in the mathematics classroom and beyond. *Review of Research in Education, 32,* 187.

National Governors Association & Council of Chief State School Officers. (2010). *Common core state standards for English language arts and literacy in history/social studies and science.* Washington, DC: Author.

Neuman, S. (2009). *Changing the odds for children at risk: Seven essential principles of educational programs that break the cycle of poverty.* Westport, CT: Praeger.

Neuman, S. B. (2003) From rhetoric to reality: The case for high-quality prekindergarten programs. *Phi Delta Kappan, 85*(4), 286–291.

Olsen, D. A. (2001, September 1). It's time to stop Head Start. *Human Events.* New York: Cato Institute.

Ornstein, A. C., & Levine, D. U. (2008). *Foundations of education* (10th ed.). Boston, MA: Houghton Mifflin.

Parsley, D., Dean, C., & Eck, J. (2005). *The power of data: Participant's manual.* Denver, CO: McREL.

Patall, E. A., Cooper, H., & Robinson, J. C. (2008). The effects of choice on intrinsic motivation and related outcomes: A meta-analysis of research findings. *Psychological Bulletin, 134*, 270–300.

Payne, C. M. (2008). *So much reform, so little change: The persistence of failure in urban schools.* Cambridge, MA: Harvard Education Press.

Pianta, R. C., Belsky, J., Houts, R., & Morrison, F. (2007, March). Opportunities to learn in America's elementary classrooms. *Science, 315*, 1795.

Pink, D. (2010). *Drive: The surprising truth about what motivates us.* New York: Riverhead Books.

Pitler, H., with Goodwin, B. (2008, Summer). Classroom observations: Learning to the see the forest *and* the trees. *Changing Schools, 58*, 19–21.

Public Impact. (2007). *School turnarounds: A review of the cross-sector evidence on dramatic organizational improvement.* Lincoln, IL: Public Impact, Academic Development Institute.

Quinn, J., & Dryfoos, J. (2009). Freeing teachers to teach: Students in full-service community schools are ready to learn. *American Educator, 33*(2), 16–21.

Ravitch, D. (2010, November 11). The myth of charter schools. *New York Review of Books, 57*(17). Retrieved from http://www.nybooks.com/articles/archives/2010/nov/11/myth-charter-schools/

Reason, J. (2000). Human error: Models and management. BMJ, *320*, 768–770.

Rice, D., & Barone, S. J. (2000). Critical periods of vulnerability for the developing nervous system: Evidence from humans and animal models. *Environmental Health Perspectives, 108*, 511–533.

Robinson, V. M. J., Lloyd, C. A., & Rowe, K. J. (2008). The impact of leadership on student outcomes: An analysis of the differential effects of leadership types. *Educational Administration Quarterly, 44*(5), 635–674.

Rosenthal, R., & Jacobson, L. (1992). *Pygmalion in the classroom.* Expanded ed. New York: Irvington.

Roth, M. (2009, December 10). Learning, adaptation can change brain connections, CMU researchers say. *Pittsburgh Post Gazette.* Retrieved from http://www.post-gazette.com/pg/09344/1019898-115.stm#ixzz0bsMOKpjH

Rothstein, R., (2004). *Class and schools: Using social, economic, and educational reform to close the black–white achievement gap.* New York: Teachers College, Columbia University.

Rothstein, R. (2010). *How to fix our schools: It's more complicated, and more work, than the Klein-Rhee "manifesto" wants you to believe.* Economic Policy Institute Policy Brief #286. Washington, DC: Economic Policy Institute.

Rouse, C. (2005, September). *The labor market consequences of an inadequate education.* Princeton University and NBER. Prepared for the Equity Symposium, "The Social Costs of Inadequate Education," Teachers' College, Columbia University.

Sanders, T., & Palka, M. K. (2009, August 6). Students taking Advanced Placement have tripled in Duval County, but more fail. *Jacksonville Times Union.* Retrieved from http://jacksonville.com/news/metro/schools/2009-05-03/story/students_taking_advanced_placement_have_tripled_in_duval_county_

Sanders, W. L., & Rivers, J. C. (1996). *Cumulative and residual effects of teachers on future academic achievement.* Knoxville: University of Tennessee Value-Added Research and Assessment Center.

Schmidt, W. H., McKnight, C. C., Cogan, L. S., Jakwerth, P. M., & Houang, R. T. (1999). *Facing the consequences: Using TIMMS for a closer look at U.S. mathematics and science education.* Dordrecht, the Netherlands: Kluwer Academic Publishers.

Schmoker, M. (1996). *Results: The key to continuous improvement.* Alexandria, VA: ASCD.

Schunk, D. H. (2005). Commentary on self-regulation in school contexts. *Learning and Instruction, 15,* 173–177.

Schweinhart, L. J. (2004). *The High/Scope Perry preschool study through age 40: Summary, conclusions, and frequently asked questions.* Ypsilanti, MI: High/Scope Educational Research Foundation.

Seligman, M. E. P. (1990). *Learned optimism: How to change your mind and your life.* New York: Pocket Books.

Senechal, M., & Young, L. (2008). The effect of family literacy interventions on children's acquisition of reading from kindergarten to grade 3: A meta-analytic review. *Review of Educational Research, 78*(4), 880–907.

Shih, G. (2010, July 22). Emeryville may point the way up. *The New York Times.* Retrieved from http://www.nytimes.com/2010/07/23/us/23bcemeryville.html?_r=2&pagewanted=print

Sizer, T. (1992a). *Horace's compromise: The dilemma of the American high school.* New York: Houghton Mifflin.

Sizer, T. (1992b). *Horace's school: Redesigning the American high school.* New York: Houghton Mifflin Company.

Southern Region Education Board. (2009a). *Combining academic and technical studies to prepare students for college and careers.* Atlanta, GA: Author.

Southern Region Education Board. (2009b). *Ready for tomorrow: Six proven ideas to graduate and prepare more students for college and 21st-century careers.* Atlanta: Author.

Steutel, J., & Spiecker, B. (2004). Cultivating sentimental dispositions through Aristotelian habituation. *Journal of Philosophy of Education, 38*(4), 531–549.

Stone, B. J., & Urquhart, V. (2008). *Remove limits to learning with systematic vocabulary instruction.* Denver, CO: McREL.

Storch, S. A., & Whitehurst, G. J. (2002). Oral language and code-related precursors to reading: Evidence from a longitudinal structural model. *Developmental Psychology, 38*, 934–947.

Stringfield, S., Reynolds, D., & Schaffer, G. (2010). *Toward highly reliable, high quality public schooling.* Paper presented at the McREL Best in the World Consortium Meeting, Denver, CO.

Suskind, R. (1998). *A hope in the unseen: An American odyssey from the inner city to the Ivy League.* New York: Broadway Books.

Temple, J. (2008, September 21). Wells Fargo sees opportunities in economy woes. *San Francisco Chronicle*, C-1.

Tomlinson, C. A. (1999). *The differentiated classroom: Responding to the needs of all learners.* Alexandria, VA: ASCD.

Tomlinson, C. A., & Cunningham Eidson, C. (2003). *Differentiation in practice: A resource guide for differentiating curriculum, grades K–5.* Alexandria, VA: ASCD.

Tomlinson, C. A., Moon, T. R., & Callahan, C. M. (1998). How well are we addressing academic diversity in the middle school? *Middle School Journal, 29*(3), 3–11.

Torgesen, J. K. (2004). Preventing early reading failure—and its devastating downward spiral: The evidence for early intervention. *American Educator, 28*(3), 6–19.

Tough, P. (2009). *Whatever it takes: Geoffrey Canada's quest to change Harlem and America.* Boston: Houghton Mifflin.

U.S. Department of Education. (2008). *Foundations for success: The final report of the National Mathematics Advisory Panel.* Washington, DC: National Mathematics Advisory Panel.

Useem, E., Offenberg, R., & Farley, E. (2007). *Closing the teacher quality gap in Philadelphia: New hope and old hurdles.* Philadelphia, PA: Research for Action.

Vygotsky, L. S. (1978). *Mind in society: Development of higher psychological processes.* Cambridge, MA: Harvard University Press.

Waters, J. T., & Marzano, R. J. (2006). *School district leadership that works: The effect of superintendent leadership on student achievement.* Denver, CO: McREL.

Waters, J. T., Marzano, R. J., & McNulty, B. A. (2003). *Balanced leadership: What 30 years of research tells us about the effect of leadership on student achievement.* Aurora, CO: McREL.

Webber, M., Carpiniello, K., Oruwariye, T., Lo, Y., Burton, W., & Appel, D. (2003). Burden of asthma in inner-city elementary schoolchildren: Do school-based health centers make a difference? *Archives of Pediatrics and Adolescent Medicine, 157*(2), 118–119.

Weick, K. E., & Sutcliffe, K. M. (2001). *Managing the unexpected: Assuring high performance in an age of complexity.* San Francisco: Jossey-Bass.

Weisberg, D., Sexton, S., Mulhern, J., & Keeling, D. (2009). *The widget effect: Our national failure to acknowledge and act on differences in teacher effectiveness.* New York: New Teacher Project.

Welch, J., & Welch, S. (2005). *Winning.* New York: Harper Business.

What Works Clearinghouse. (2007). *Direct Instruction, DISTAR, and Language for Learning: What Works Clearinghouse intervention report.* Washington, DC: U.S. Department of Education, Institute of Education Sciences.

What Works Clearinghouse. (2009). *Assisting students struggling with reading: Response to Intervention (RtI) and multi-tier intervention in the primary grades.* Washington, DC: U.S. Department of Education, Institute of Education Sciences.

White, K. R. (1982). The relationship between socioeconomic status and academic achievement. *Psychological Bulletin, 91*(3), 470.

Whitehurst, G. J. (1997). Language processes in context: Language learning in children reared in poverty. In L. B. Adamson & M. A. Romski (Eds.), *Research on communication and language disorders: Contribution to theories of language development* (pp. 233–266). Baltimore, MD: Brookes.

Whitman, D. (2008). An appeal to authority: The new paternalism in urban schools. *Education Next, 8*(4), 53–58.

Wiggins, G., & McTighe, J. (1998). *Understanding by Design.* Alexandria, VA: Association for Supervision and Curriculum Development.

Willingham, D. T. (2009). *Why don't students like school? A cognitive psychologist answers questions about how the mind works and what it means for the classroom.* San Francisco: Jossey Bass.

Wolmar, C. (1994, June 20). Air disaster averted by collision alert device: Near-miss adds to case for US system. *UK Independent.* Retrieved from http://www.independent.co.uk/news/uk/air-disaster-averted-by-collision-alert-device-nearmiss-adds-to-case-for-us-system-1423773.html?cmp=ilc-n

Wood, D., Bruner, J. C., & Ross, G. (1976). The role of tutoring in problem solving. *Journal of Child Psychology and Psychiatry, 17*, 89–100.

Zehr, M. A. (2010, January 27). Tailoring lessons for English-learners: A California district gets results, and recognition, using "Response to Intervention." *Education Week, 29*(19), 1, 10.

Index

Note: Information presented in figures is denoted by *f*.

About the Author

Bryan Goodwin is Vice President of Communications and Marketing at Mid-continent Research for Education and Learning (McREL), a Denver-based nonprofit education research and development organization. For the past 13 years at McREL, he has been responsible for writing and editing numerous articles, reports, and research briefs and serves as chief editor of the McREL magazine, *Changing Schools*. In 2009, he played a key role in McREL's 40-person effort to review and analyze hundreds of research reports on effective school and district practices into a series of eight in-depth reports, which Goodwin distilled into the report *Changing the Odds for Student Success: What Matters Most*. It serves as the foundation for this book. In addition to his McREL publications, Goodwin writes a regular column on educational research for ASCD's *Educational Leadership* magazine and served as lead author of the book *The Future of Schooling: Educating America in 2020* (Solution Tree Press, 2010). Prior to his work at McREL, Goodwin taught high school in St. Croix, U.S. Virgin Islands, and worked as a newspaper reporter in the Virgin Islands and Pennsylvania. He has a bachelor's degree in English–Professional Writing from Baylor University in Waco, Texas, and a master's degree in Rhetoric and Communications from the University of Virginia in Charlottesville, Virginia.

About McREL

Mid-continent Research for Education and Learning (McREL) is a nationally recognized, nonprofit education research and development organization, headquartered in Denver, Colorado, with offices in Honolulu, Hawaii and Omaha, Nebraska. Since 1966, McREL has helped translate research and professional wisdom about what works in education into practical guidance for educators. Our 120-plus staff members and affiliates include respected researchers, experienced consultants, and published writers who provide educators with research-based guidance, consultation, and professional development for improving student outcomes.

The What Matters Most System Survey

See how well your school or district is addressing the *Simply Better* "touchstones" with the What Matters Most System Survey at survey. changetheodds.org. Take the free, 20-minute quiz to identify your school or district's strengths as well as areas where focused improvements are likely to change the odds for student success.